W9-CXV-189

Interpretation
S K I L L S :
American
Sign Language
to English

by Marty M. Taylor Ph.D.

A publication of Interpreting Consolidated
Box 203, Main P.O., Edmonton, Alberta, Canada T5J 2J1

**INTERPRETING
CONSOLIDATED**

Copyright © 2002, by Marty M. Taylor, Ph.D.

All rights reserved. No part of this publication may be reproduced, stored in a retrieval system, or transmitted, in any form or by any means, electronic, mechanical, photocopying, recording, or otherwise, without the written consent of Interpreting Consolidated. Requests for permission or further information should be addressed to Interpreting Consolidated, Box 203, Main P.O., Edmonton, Alberta, Canada T5J 2J1

Edited by Amanda Leslie-Spinks
Cover design and layout by Perry Shulak

www.aslinterpreting.com

Printed, bound and published in Canada

National Library of Canada Cataloguing in Publication Data

Taylor, Marty M., date
  Interpretation skills: American sign language to English

Includes bibliographical references and index.
Interpreters for the deaf
ISBN 0-9697792-4-0

  1. Interpreters for the deaf. 2. American Sign Language. I. Title.

HV2474.T378 2002   419   C2002-900059-9

Dedication

I can directly attribute the success of my professional career to three very important individuals. They are, in the order in which they entered my life:

o Theresa B. Smith, my first instructor of interpreting, who set a high standard for ASL/English interpretation that she herself continues to model exceptionally well.

o Sharon Neumann Solow, my second instructor of interpreting, and the first person who taught me how to teach. She was excellent at separating the complicated task of teaching into manageable steps, which was especially necessary for me as I began my teaching career when I was young and inexperienced.

o Virginia Hughes, my first employer in the interpreting profession, who taught me the benefit of graduate education, encouraging me to go beyond a B.A. She was so right!

All three of these women have been my mentors, my supporters and my friends. They have maintained their active involvement in the interpreting profession for decades. They are exceptional interpreters and educators who are always on the cutting edge of our field.

I thank these three strong and progressive women with all my heart!

Table of Contents

Table of Contents

Definition of Terms

Major Features

Comprehension: ASL Lexicon

Comprehension: ASL Discourse

Production: English Lexicon

Acknowledgements

Since my research was conducted over a seven-year period (1995-2001), there are many people and organizations that I would like to thank.

Firstly, 44 deaf and non-deaf educators reviewed the research at various stages in the pilot studies and expert panels in Canada and the United States. Without their extensive feedback, the work would not contain the depth that it currently has. Their input was invaluable and their willingness to participate in the reviews is greatly appreciated.

Secondly, the many friends, too many to mention here, who were always willing to ask how "book #2" was progressing and listened to my ever present writing and research woes. I especially want to mention Tanya Adler, Brenda Nicodemus and my mother, Bernie Taylor.

I would like to thank the individual interpreters and the Association of Visual Language Interpreters of Canada (AVLIC) for allowing me to use their national certification examination videotapes (1990-1995).

The Interpreter Training Program students (1995-1996) at Grant MacEwan College in Edmonton, Alberta participated and allowed me to observe them work.

The Social Sciences and Humanities Research Council of Canada (SSHRC) provided post-doctoral support which allowed me to begin the research for this textbook much earlier than I could have otherwise.

Todd Rogers and the University of Alberta provided office space and an opportunity to seek advice on a regular basis as long as I needed it.

Joseph Shaffir, Barrister and Solicitor, allowed me the use of his eleventh floor office at a very affordable price.

Finally, I would like to thank Amanda Leslie-Spinks for making the final product what it is. Her writing expertise, along with her background in languages helped to make the book not only read better, but she also clarified many murky areas. She helped me over the last hump to complete this writing.

Foreword

In the field of ASL/English interpretation little research on skills required to provide equivalency of meaning between the two languages has been done. The research behind the textbook *Interpretation Skills: English to American Sign Language* (1993) was one of the first attempts to catalogue skills and possible errors that occur in interpreting from English to ASL. The textbook is widely used throughout Canada and the United States. It is also used in other parts of the world including Australia, Malaysia, Italy, Denmark and Russia. Surveys among individuals and interpreting programs that use the textbook find it thorough and useful.

This book is intended for people working primarily from ASL to English. It identifies skills required to render ASL to English interpretations using the same research method as the first book. These two pieces of research complement each other and should be used together. Typically interpreters' strengths going from English to ASL are similar to their strengths in going from ASL to English, and the same applies to their weaknesses. In some general ways, the interpretation *process* is the same regardless of which is the source language (the language used to initiate the message) and the target language (the language used in the interpretation). However, the specific skills necessary to provide interpretations from English to ASL and from ASL to English differ. For example, if interpreting from English to ASL, the interpreter's voice quality is not applicable and therefore not assessed. Likewise when interpreting from ASL to English there would be no evaluation of an interpreter's signing; there is no signing.

In both books, the term ASL is used in its broadest sense meaning that Deaf/deaf signers may use a wide range of language from ASL native signing to a more English-based signing. This entire range of signing was included in the research. No restrictions were placed on the degree of ASL fluency.

Research Overview

Purpose

The main goal of the research was to determine patterns of successful interpretation behavior that are exhibited when working from American Sign Language (ASL) to spoken English. The objective was to develop a diagnostic assessment instrument to evaluate ASL-to-English interpretations provided by novice and expert interpreters with various levels of skills and experience.

Interpreters come from all walks of life. Some of them have opportunities for professional training, while others learn sign language and the tasks of interpretation on the job. Some interpreters are the best in their community while others are not. Some have had opportunities to travel and see what other communities of interpreters have to offer. Some are in large urban communities where support, training and workshops are offered on a regular basis, whereas others are in rural communities and perhaps only know one deaf child with whom they work.

With the multitude of factors that contribute to the abilities of interpreters, it is important to clarify the *foundational skills* and *major features* of successful interpretations. Once this framework is established, it offers a basis for objective evaluation of interpreters with different levels of experience.

This book can be used in formative or summative evaluation of interpretation work. For example, if an interpreter's work is evaluated regularly using this tool, a clear measure of skill progression will be available. Alternatively, if the assessment is carried out once at the end of a semester, or a set of workshops, it provides a summative or final evaluation of that portion of the interpreter's education.

The assessment technique is both descriptive and diagnostic. The book describes very specific skills that have been demonstrated by certified and non-certified interpreters and interpreting students in Canada and the United States. Each skill is defined by noting the specific errors that occur when that skill is <u>not</u> present. Errors associated with each skill are discussed and detailed examples of their occurrence are provided.

When the instrument is used to note patterns of errors specific to a particular piece of work, it becomes diagnostic. The existence of those patterns will often point to underlying strengths and/or weaknesses in the interpreter's skill set, which can then be targeted for retention or improvement.

Profile of Interpreters

One of the most pressing research needs is to generate a profile of the competent ASL/English interpreter which highlights major features of successful interpretation. Such a profile provides the cornerstone of future work in the areas of evaluation/certification, entrance and exit criteria for interpreting programs, labor market analysis, and curriculum and materials development.

ASL competence

Several of the current interpretation models used in the ASL/English field are process models that assume bilingualism of the interpreter (e.g., Cokely model, Colonomos model). However, current research shows a continuing and significant gap in interpreters' ability to comprehend ASL. This basic problem is present prior to any difficulty with the interpretation process itself. The ASL input, the source message, is not understood completely and thus the interpretation has no chance of being successful regardless of the interpreter's processing ability. The literature reports that if interpreters do not understand the source language they can not possibly interpret the message into a target language.

The field of interpretation continues to accept novice signers into interpreting programs. As a result, interpreting programs attempt to teach both sign language and interpreting within the same program. This diminishes students' ability to concentrate solely on their interpretation skills because they are trying simultaneously to master ASL. It is unfortunate that limited fluency in ASL is so prevalent.

Most interpreters are not native signers and therefore have acquired their ASL language skills later in life. As a result, many issues related to the comprehension of ASL by second language users continue to affect the interpreting profession and need to be addressed. Ideally, students who graduate from interpreting programs would have highly developed ASL expressive and receptive skills. However, the fact is that most graduates of interpreting programs do not have advanced competency in ASL. This is a weakness across programs in Canada and the United States. It is slowly being addressed by requiring more ASL skills for entry into interpreting programs. However, most interpreting programs continue to focus a great deal of time on developing ASL skills. As expected, the research for this book showed strong evidence of shortcomings related to ASL comprehension skills.

Variations in signing

ASL varies from person to person, and varies within geographic regions. As a result, interpreters must handle a tremendous range of signing skills. To navigate effectively in this diverse community, interpreters must possess highly developed and adaptable signing comprehension abilities. In addition, interpreters must anticipate variation in signing from male and female, young and old, professional and non-professional individuals because these factors are also part of all language production. As an added complication, there is a lack of standardized teaching of ASL to Deaf/deaf individuals.

There will be signing variations among people who have:
o   learned sign language later in life;
o   learned ASL as infants and as their first language from their Deaf parents;
o   attended residential schools;
o   attended mainstream programs;
o   had a variety of experience with different signers;
o   had contact limited to their non-signing family members and/or a single interpreter at school.

NOTE: English signing and variations of English signing are prevalent. This text will include them as much as possible. However, the primary focus is on ASL.

Levels of experience

There are differences between expert and novice interpretations. Experts tend to be more competent in both languages, English and ASL, and know how to manipulate the languages more successfully than novices. The expert also has more experience in the profession. However, both experts and novices may have some difficulty with either or both languages. If their errors are minor and infrequent, then the message is likely to come across to the audience. On the other hand, if the errors significantly skew or alter the message and are frequent, the resulting interpretation is not effective and the audience does not receive the necessary information from the signer. The level of experience of interpreters will make a difference in how well they cope with their shortcomings in either or both languages.

Methodology

The research for this book followed the steps proposed by Crocker and Algina (1986) for developing assessment instruments:
   o   determine the purpose of diagnostic assessment;
   o   determine the limitations of the diagnostic instrument;
   o   review available literature;
   o   conduct task analysis;
   o   conduct error analysis;
   o   carry out pilot studies; and,
   o   submit results to an expert panel review.

Purpose

The primary purpose of the research was to develop a diagnostic assessment instrument to assess ASL-to-English interpretations provided by novice and expert interpreters with various levels of skills and experience.

Literature review

The text is based on research currently available in the areas of interpretation, discourse and public speaking skills. It includes the expertise of interpreters and interpreter educators, as well as audiences, both Deaf/deaf and non-deaf who rely on interpretation from time to time. Literature used to prepare *Interpretation Skills: English to ASL* was reconsidered. Research conducted on interpretation skills since 1993 was collected and analyzed with particular attention to work on ASL-to-English interpretation.

Task and error analyses

Live and videotaped interpretations/transliterations were analyzed. A total of 182 live interpretations were viewed at local, national and international venues. Approximately 45 percent involved Canadian interpreters working in Canada, 45 percent were Americans working in the United States, and approximately 10 percent were Canadian and American interpreters working in ASL/English in other countries. This latter group included interpreters who either resided in the foreign country or were brought from Canada and the United States to provide interpretation for Canadian and American delegates to international events.

Of the 182 live interpretations viewed, 104 were the work of interpreters who had national certification from Canada – the Certificate of Interpretation (COI) from the Association of Visual Language Interpreters of Canada (AVLIC) – or from the United States – the Comprehensive Skills Certificate (CSC), or the Certificate of Interpretation (CI) and the Certificate of Transliteration (CT) from the Registry of Interpreters for the Deaf (RID). Some interpreters had AVLIC and RID. There were 62 interpreters who were not nationally certified, *and* 16 whose certification was unknown at the time.

The total number of videotaped interpretations analyzed was 244. Of these, 75 were from candidates for the AVLIC Test of Interpretation – both successful and unsuccessful. A further 128 were student interpreters who were not certified and were currently enrolled in interpreter programs in Canada and the United States, and 46 were interpreters on videotapes available to the public. Their certification status at the time of the taping was not noted in all cases. Among those specifying certification status, approximately 30 percent were nationally certified by AVLIC, RID or both.

When possible, the source text was included in the research materials. Analysis was based on a visual record of the signer, the voice of the interpreter producing the target message and a verbatim transcription of the English interpretation. In this way the lag time, that is, the interpreter's processing time, could be assessed.

Pilot studies and expert panel reviews

Two pilot studies were conducted in Alberta. Three expert panel reviews were conducted in Minnesota, Oregon and Colorado. A total of 44 deaf and non-deaf people were involved in the reviews. All of them were from Canada and the United States and had two to thirty-five years of experience teaching interpreters. They were either nationally certified interpreters in Canada or the United States, or certified instructors with ASLTA (American Sign Language Teachers Association).

After each line-by-line review, the panelists' comments were documented and incorporated into the successive versions of the instrument.

It was agreed by all reviewers that interpreters had problems with the source language, ASL, and this affected the interpretation outcome, separately from skills in the interpretation process. First and foremost, interpreters must be fluent in ASL and English.

Results

The significant amount of data collected, made it possible to develop a useful diagnostic assessment tool to categorize ASL-to-English interpretation skills and their possible associated errors. These include skills at lexical and at discourse levels. The lexical level refers to knowledge of individual signs and English words. The discourse level refers to elements of meaning expressed when lexical units are joined into phrases, sentences, paragraphs and entire texts.

The research led to identification of six major features of interpretation from ASL to English:
- o two pertain to ASL comprehension
  - comprehension: ASL lexicon
  - comprehension: ASL discourse
- o three pertain to English production and delivery
  - production: English lexicon
  - production: English discourse
  - delivery: public speaking
- o one pertains to the image the interpreter projects
  - composure and appearance

ASL comprehension

The research for the textbook, *Interpretation Skills: English to American Sign Language,* showed ASL competency was a key area of concern. The same phenomenon showed clearly in the 1995 - 2001 research, which provided evidence that many interpretation errors were due to lack of comprehension of the source language, ASL. Therefore, effectiveness and accuracy in the interpretation needed to be analyzed in relation to the signing comprehension skills of the interpreter.

Analysis of the research material showed that accuracy of interpretation was affected by factors like the speed with which ASL was delivered, the signing style of the signer, such as left-handedness, and regional differences between signer and interpreter.

The lack of ASL comprehension that appeared regularly in the research, made it clear that ASL lexicon and ASL discourse are two important features of interpretation that need to be addressed in analysis and assessment.

English production and delivery

The research showed that skill levels in the production and delivery of spoken English varied among the interpretations analyzed. The better the command of English at both the lexical and discourse levels, the better the final product. Lack of public speaking skills also impacted the effectiveness of the interpretation.

Interpreter's image

Listeners can grasp the signer's message most easily when the interpreter's appearance and mannerisms are not distracting. For example, an interpreter may be frowning with concentration even while interpreting a joke. In the research samples this kind of inappropriate addition of information occurred frequently.

Categorizing knowledge-lean and knowledge-rich skills

The research lead to an analysis of the interpretation process in terms of knowledge-lean and knowledge-rich skills. "Knowledge-lean" skills are basic and fundamental language skills. In the ASL-to-English interpretation process, knowledge-lean skills are related to ASL comprehension at the lexical and discourse level. Basic knowledge of English at the lexical level is also a knowledge-lean interpretation skill. These three kinds of lean skill must be present before an interpreter can move to complex interpretation tasks.

"Knowledge rich" refers to context-sensitive interpretation skills that allow an interpreter to communicate the subtle differences in meaning and tone that the signer is expressing. Knowledge-rich skills give access to a more complex level of meaning than verbatim (word for word) interpretations. English production at the discourse level, delivery, and composure and appearance are all knowledge-rich skills.

An example of knowledge-lean and knowledge-rich skills can be drawn from the field of construction. A building can not be constructed before an appropriate site is located, a plan is drawn, materials are gathered and qualified workers are available. These preparatory steps are knowledge-lean, or foundational skills. Only with such resources in place can the actual construction begin. The final product and the quality of the completed construction depend on the overall expertise – knowledge rich skills – contributed during each step of the process. For example, if the site is too small for the building planned, then the entire project will be weak and the outcome less than desirable. If, on the other hand, the site is well chosen, the architectural plan is suitable to the site (e.g., appropriate to the neighborhood in terms of appearance and size), if the materials are of good quality, and the workers are highly skilled, then the final structure will be well made.

MAJOR FEATURES	COMPLEXITY LEVEL
o Comprehension: ASL lexicon o Comprehension: ASL discourse o Production: English lexicon	KNOWLEDGE-LEAN SKILLS
o Production: English discourse o Delivery: public speaking o Composure and appearance	KNOWLEDGE-RICH SKILLS

Relationship to the Textbook, *Interpretation Skills: English to ASL*

Similarities

When the original research was conducted for *Interpretation Skills: English to ASL*, it was recognized that ASL-to-English interpretation uses similar skills but requires a different diagnostic approach. For this discussion of ASL-to-English interpretation new data was collected. The same research methodology was used for each text. A literature review was done; a task and error analysis was conducted of live and videotaped interpretations; and finally, pilot studies and expert panel reviews were done.

The most significant finding in both pieces of research was that many of the errors demonstrated in the interpretation samples were caused by deficiencies in interpreters' ASL skills. When interpreting from English to ASL, it was ASL signing skills that were lacking. With ASL-to-English interpretation, it was ASL comprehension skills that were lacking.

Differences

The layout used for describing the skills and possible errors was altered from the first to the second text for ease of use. Each skill has been bolded for quick access.

An Inclusive Approach

In providing effective assessments, it is helpful to use inclusive concepts and definitions. They most accurately capture the range of work interpreters encounter and provide a basis for shared understanding. This text uses the most inclusive approach possible:

1) Interpretation and transliteration are both included under the general term "interpretation." In parts of the United States, people differentiate between transliterating and interpreting. "Transliteration" is used to refer to an English-like process like contact signing, PSE (Pidgin Signed English), CASE (Conceptually Accurate Signed English) and signed English, whereas "interpretation" is used to mean moving between two different languages (e.g., English and ASL, French and Spanish). Whether the signer used more English- or more ASL-based expressions, or switched between these two on an English-ASL continuum, the task of the interpreter is referred to as interpretation.

2) The research on ASL-to-English interpretation includes all forms of American Sign Language and English variations of signing, including those referred to as (e.g., contact signing, CASE, PSE, signed English). No distinction is made among the variety of ways deaf people express themselves in sign language.

3) The interpretation has to agree with the signer's message whether it is presented in ASL, CASE, PSE or signed English. No comment is made on whether the D/deaf people's signing is native ASL, or signed English or a combination. It is all unequivocally accepted as source text.

4) Interpreters and interpreting students have different experiences and backgrounds, as well as different levels of skill. These factors do not necessarily correspond to certification level or the number of years interpreters have been working. At any time, depending on the setting, the audience, and the interpreter's familiarity with the people involved and the topic discussed, an interpreter may be an expert or a novice.

Restrictions on the Research

With all research it is important to delineate what the research was and what it was not, what it included and what it did not.

This research considered the outcome of the interpretation process, those behaviors that were successful and those that were not. It focused solely on the final English product, and how closely it relayed the signer's message and intent.

The research looked at product only, without any attempt to interview interpreters. They were not asked about world knowledge, interpersonal skills, ethical decision making (e.g., discretion), cultural sensitivity or their impression of their own work. Although all of these issues are important and vital for providing dynamically equivalent interpretations, they were beyond the scope of this research.

The present text provides a profile of the competent interpreter on the basis of observable skills. Only consistent patterns in the actual production and delivery of an interpretation, and the relationship of errors as they related to the ASL source text, ASL lexicon and ASL discourse were included as part of an assessment.

Because the research focused on the product and not the process of interpretation, the reasons for errors were not addressed. The diagnostic use of the tool will point to underlying skill weaknesses but offers no conclusions about their source or what should be done to correct them. It is up to interpreters and educators to determine the reasons an interpretation is faulty. Is it their processing abilities? Is it their ASL receptive skills? Or is it nervousness that caused unsuccessful patterns in the interpretation? These are important topics for future research.

All of the signers captured live or on videotape were presenting to an audience in a lecture format. Some audiences were primarily hearing/non-deaf, and some were primarily deaf with only a few hearing/non-deaf individuals present. Interaction between the signer and the audience was not possible and therefore no interpretation of discussions or questions and answers was required.

Finally, elements of the relationship between the signer and the interpreter were not addressed. These include the interpreter's ability to ask for clarification at appropriate times, or to let the signer know when more time is needed to complete interpretation of a particular section of work.

Recommendations for Future Research

The research effort is continuous. As more aspects of interpretation are researched and reported, the field of interpretation will be enhanced.

This text makes a start on research that needs to be done in the vast area of interpretation. It begins to answer the question of what makes ASL-to-English interpretation effective? Specifically, it focuses on message equivalency and provides evidence and supporting examples about what is equivalent and what is not. This research provides interpreters with a solid foundation that will be useful in continuing the development of their skills.

Several possibilities for continued research are immediately evident. Now that patterns of behavior related to message equivalency have been identified, it is important to determine exactly what contributed to the success or lack of success in particular interpretations. The causes of accuracy and inaccuracy in interpretations are important and can add to the model presented here. Such work, drawing on the perceptions of interpreters and interpreting students would offer a deeper understanding of the intricate task of interpretation. Once reasons behind the success or lack of success are determined, specific solutions can be developed.

Some of the questions that need to be asked in future research are:

o   What core skills will predict the success of the interpretation as a whole?

o   What is the relation between interpreter language competencies assessed by this model and the bilingual fluency presupposed in other models (e.g., Cokely and Colonomos)?

o   What is "too much" interpretation? When does a cultural interpretation or a contextualized interpretation go too far?

o   How can data on interpreter thought processes – collected by research interviews – help to pinpoint the source of interpretation errors in source and target language competency.

o   What differences exist between interpretations performed simultaneously and those performed consecutively?

Intended Audience

The ultimate goal of the text is to assist interpreters in improving their interpretation accuracy by documenting effective and ineffective patterns observed in their work. Readers with a thorough grounding in ASL, spoken English and interpretation will be able to make best use of its content.

It will benefit both Deaf and non-deaf people who are:
- o   interpreting students
- o   interpreting practitioners
- o   interpreter educators
- o   interpretation researchers

This textbook is meant for individuals who are interested in understanding the complexity of the interpretation task and for those who are interested in acquiring knowledge about how to analyze their own work and the work of others.

Organization of the Text

This textbook consists of the introductory pages describing the background of the research and the organization of the text, six Major Features of ASL-to-English interpretation, Professional Organizations, Bibliography and Subject Index.

Each Major Feature begins with an overview of the section. Following this brief introduction, the skills and their associated possible errors are listed and described using examples and a narrative to deepen understanding of each skill and error.

The same error may be mentioned in more than one place in the book. This redundancy is intentional. For example, errors related to the use of non-manual markers are discussed in connection with ASL lexical features and also with ASL discourse features. The subject index in the back of the book will direct readers to all references to a particular skill or error. Readers may find it helpful to recognize that patterns of ineffective behaviors recur in more than one skill area. Readers should focus on how common errors impact on each skill with which they are associated. Although an error may be described in different places in the book, the context in which errors are discussed is important.

Key for Reading ASL Gloss

The conventions used in *Interpretation Skills: English to ASL* are also used in this text. To date there is no standardized way to write ASL. However there are some well recognized techniques used to convey ASL in written form:

o   ASL signs will be written using English words (glosses). These words will be capitalized. For example, the sign for "house" will be written HOUSE. If more than one house is indicated, then plus signs (i.e., ++) will be used to indicate plural, or the repetition of the sign.

o   When more than one English word is required to convey the meaning of a sign, the writing will include the English glosses for the sign joined by hyphens to indicate it is all one sign. For example, DRIVE-UP-HILL, refers to one sign that was used to express not only the meaning of "drive" but also "driving up hill."

o   Words that are fingerspelled will be written with a hyphen between each letter. Again all of the letters will be capitalized. For example, the ASL written format for "Martina" will be M-A-R-T-I-N-A.

o   Classifiers will be written with the abbreviation, CL, followed by the handshape and the meaning like CL:3 "vehicle" and CL:1 "person."

o   Commas will be used to indicate a pause in ASL.

o   Loan signs will be written with a hatchmark (#) in front of the sign like #BANK, #DOG and #EARLY.

o   Compound signs will be written with a semi circle attaching the signs that form the compound sign like BLACK⌢NAME meaning "bad reputation."

25

o   When the interpretation examples include English words, phrases or sentences, these English elements will appear in quotation marks. For example, if the interpretation was "Juan is a champion hockey player" the exact words used will be in quotes.

Definition of Terms

Source and target languages

The **source language** is ASL in its broadest form. This includes texts where signers use ASL, PSE, or a contact variety of signing. ASL, for the purposes of this research includes everything except signing systems that were developed to teach English to children such as SEE and LOVE. A **source message** is a particular communication produced by a signer in the source language.

The **target language** in this context is spoken English. A **target message** is a particular English interpretation produced by an interpreter from the source message.

Categories of errors

Unsuccessful interpretation behaviors can be called errors, miscues, mistakes or inaccurate work. Any part of a message that is not equivalent in meaning to the source message is considered an error. Errors fall into two distinct categories: frequent errors and severe errors.

Frequency refers to the number of times an error occurs. Low frequency errors occur seldom or occasionally, perhaps once or twice. High frequency errors occur repeatedly.

Severity refers to the degree of inaccuracy and the potential for misunderstanding caused. If an error does not skew the meaning, it is considered low severity. "Skewing" is defined as anything that is omitted from the source message or added to the target interpretation that was not present in the source message. If the error skews the meaning and the source message is not retrievable or its meaning is greatly altered, the error is severe. For example, an interpretation contains many repairs – the interpreter corrects him or herself after saying, "Oh, I meant…." This error may be frequent, but is not severe because the audience can retrieve the signer's message, assuming that the repairs are accurate. If, however, statements are interpreted as questions, then this error is severe because the source message and intent are conveyed inaccurately and are not retrievable.

It is crucial to remember that the goal of the interpretation is message equivalency. What the signer conveys to the Deaf/deaf audience should be what the interpreter conveys to the non-deaf audience.

Comprehension:
ASL Lexicon

OVERVIEW

Research consistently documents that interpreters have difficulty comprehending ASL. This section focuses on one of the fundamental skill groupings in the interpretation process, command of ASL lexicon.

This assessment instrument does not include the ideas and perceptions of interpreters about their own work. As a result, evaluations that are developed from it can not determine precisely whether weak equivalency in interpretation is due to interpreter's lack of comprehension of ASL or problems in production of English. Only the interpreter can articulate the exact reason for his or her difficulty. However, once diagnostic assessment of this skill grouping is completed, there will be some indication if the challenge facing the interpreter is comprehension of ASL. Errors associated with ASL lexical skills are documented in this section. As a group they provide a template for assessing patterns in the work being considered.

1. Fingerspelling is interpreted accurately.

Possible errors

1a. Fingerspelled words are omitted or partially omitted: O-T-T-O S-H-A-W-A-R-T-Z is spelled and only "Otto" is interpreted.

1b. When fingerspelling is rapid, the interpretation is inaccurate: The signer spells W-E-S-T-J-E-T fast and the interpreter conveys "Western."

1c. When fingerspelling is slow, the interpretation is inaccurate: The fingerspelling is slowed for emphasis and the interpretation does not convey the additional emphasis.

1d. Lexicalized fingerspelling (i.e., loan signs) is interpreted inaccurately: #B-A-C-K is signed and the interpreter says, "bank."

1e. When partial fingerspelling is present, the interpretation is inaccurate: The signer explains about having a shot in the lower back to block the pain during childbirth and fingerspells

33

E-P-I-D..., the interpreter is not able to complete the word and say "epidural."

1f. When the signer doesn't use mouth movements, the interpretation is inaccurate.

1g. When the signer's mouth movements are different from standard English mouth movements, the interpretation is inaccurate: "Ph.D." which is commonly voiced as three individual letters in spoken English, "p" "h" "d," is mouthed as "FUD" by the signer and conveyed as "fud" instead of "p" "h" "d" by the interpreter.

Discussion

Signers will choose to fingerspell certain concepts for reasons such as emphasis, specificity, contrast and even to assist interpreters with technical jargon.

The interpreter's ability to comprehend fingerspelling has a significant impact on the effectiveness of the interpretation. Fingerspelled words such as proper names (e.g., Jose, Taiwan, or Vaseline) most often need to be retained in the interpretation. If the meaning is lost or skewed because the precise meaning of the fingerspelling was not interpreted into English, then errors are present in the interpretation. There can be several causes of ineffectiveness:

o   the interpreter did not understand the fingerspelling;

o   the interpreter determined incorrectly that the information was not crucial for conveying the equivalent message in English; or,

o   there was no opportunity to ask for clarification because the signer was on videotape.

Whatever the difficulties, the interpretation must convey a dynamically equivalent message, and failure to do so, indicates errors are present. Not all fingerspelled words will be interpreted literally into English, however the meaning attributed by the signer to the fingerspelling must be conveyed.

1a.   Fingerspelled words are omitted or partially omitted.

Difficulty may occur when several fingerspelled words are signed consecutively, for instance, during roll call in a classroom or in an English passage from archaic English text like a Shakespeare play. In these situations, the interpreter may not understand all of the fingerspelled words, may be unable to remember them or unable to articulate them as fast as they are produced. Whatever the case, omissions or errors will be present in the work.

When fingerspelling is used on both hands either simultaneously or consecutively, the signer's intent can be misinterpreted. For example, simultaneously fingerspelling O-F-F on the right and left hands, can mean "a relationship broke up." However, the interpreter might convey "of." Or, if consecutive fingerspelling is used with I-N-F-O-R-M-A-L spelled on the dominant hand, and then F-O-R-M-A-L spelled on the non-dominant hand, one or both of these concepts may be omitted or misinterpreted.

1b.   When fingerspelling is rapid, the interpretation is inaccurate.

At times, fingerspelling is missed because it is delivered in a rapid manner that the interpreter fails to comprehend and/or interpret. For example, the signer is talking about his new condo purchase and the amenities available in the complex, such as a pool, sauna and exercise room. The fingerspelling is rapid for P-O-O-L and S-A-U-N-A because he is excited about taking advantage of these facilities in his building. The interpreter may get left behind.

1c.   When fingerspelling is slow, the interpretation is inaccurate.

At other times, inaccuracies occur because the fingerspelling is slow. It may be articulated at reduced pace for emphatic purposes and the interpreter does not comprehend the emphasis. For example, the signer is underlining the fact that she lives on Magnolia, and not on Queen Anne hill in Seattle. The fact that she lives on Magnolia is important to her and thus she spells it at a slower pace than her other fingerspelled words. The interpreter misses the emphatic distinction.

1d.   Lexicalized fingerspelling (i.e., loan signs) is interpreted inaccurately.

Another area of difficulty often observed in the research samples was inability to comprehend and interpret lexicalized fingerspelling, or loan signs as they are commonly referred to in the literature, such as #STYLE, #EARLY and #BANK. These are fingerspelled words that are signed in such a way as to become a lexical item in themselves. Technically speaking they are not fingerspelling, but ASL signs made from borrowed vocabulary. They are produced by making individual letters with certain standardized movements and in specific locations. Interpreters may perceive #BANK as "back" or confuse #EARLY with the name "Sally".

1e.   When partial fingerspelling is present, the interpretation is inaccurate.

Signers have varying degrees of ability to use the English language. When fingerspelling English words, especially uncommon words, partial spellings may be produced. In reading partial fingerspelling, the interpreter may substitute a word that is inaccurate for the context. For instance, the signer spells E-P-I-D meaning "epidural" and the interpreter says, "epidermis." Technical terms associated with the legal system such as "prosecutor" and "defendant" may be signed and part of the words may be spelled as well. It is up to the interpreter to render the complete interpretation. It is not the deaf person's responsibility to provide the English words for the interpreter.

1f. When the signer doesn't use mouth movements, the interpretation is inaccurate.

When signers do not mouth words, especially when fingerspelling, it can cause difficulty for some interpreters. If the interpreter relies on mouthing and either mouthing is not present or it is sporadic, then errors may occur in the interpretation.

1g. When the signer's mouth movements are different from standard English mouth movements, the interpretation is inaccurate.

Signers may mouth words differently from the way they are produced by native English speakers. For example, signers sometimes mouth English words such as "Thomas" and "Thailand" with a "TH" at the beginning of the words. When interpreters are not familiar with differences between spoken English and ASL, errors can easily occur. Interpreters may think that they misunderstood the spelling because of the use of different mouthing. In fact, they may have understood the spelling but are not compensating for this difference between native-English users and signers' mouthing.

2. Numbers like ratios, ages and fractions are interpreted accurately.

Possible errors

2a. Numbers are omitted or partially omitted: The signer specifies the age of a child and the interpretation does not.
2b. When numbers are produced rapidly, the interpretation is inaccurate: FIVE-PERCENT is signed and "50 percent" is interpreted.
2c. When numbers are produced slowly, the interpretation is inaccurate: The number is signed slowly for emphasis and the interpretation does not convey the emphasis.

2d. Numbering systems are interpreted inaccurately: "Five-dollars" is interpreted when FIFTH-PLACE is signed.

2e. When number incorporation is used, the interpretation is inaccurate: TWO-HOUR is signed and "one hour" is interpreted.

Discussion

2a.   Numbers are omitted or partially omitted.

When numbers are omitted, two types of errors can occur. First, the entire number or part of the number is missing from the English target message. Saying only "19" for the signed number NINETEEN -FIFTY-FIVE is considered an omission. Saying only part of an address rather than the complete address is also an error. Or second, the number is interpreted inaccurately. When NINETY-SIX is signed, the wrong number, "78," is voiced.

It was noted in the research samples that multi-digit numbers were often interpreted in the wrong order, either backwards or out of sequence when it came to ages, addresses and dates. For example, when a number is signed several times as in FIFTY-SIX++, the interpreter misunderstood the sequence and reversed the numbers, saying "65."

2b.   When numbers are produced rapidly, the interpretation is inaccurate.

The research also indicated that the speed with which signers produce numbers affected the accuracy of the interpretation. If numbers were produced quickly and/or in succession (i.e., a series of numbers), the inaccuracy of the interpretation increased.

Interpreters may use a considerable amount of processing time (i.e., lag time), to achieve the best target message. However it is good practice to try to reduce processing time to catch up with the signer, when numbers are signed. That way the number will not be forgotten. In general, numbers are more effectively interpreted shortly after they are signed than after a long delay. That is because numbers are often produced as isolated pieces of information (e.g., dates, addresses and budgets) which have no memory hooks to help the interpreter.

2c.   When numbers are produced slowly, the interpretation is inaccurate.

Alternatively, if numbers are articulated slowly, the interpretation may be skewed. Novel or unique information is often presented in numbers or fingerspelling produced more slowly than usual. For example, the signer emphasizes that his young brother owns THREE houses, and not only reduces the speed of signing, but also alters the manner in which he produces the number "three." This movement may start with the palm facing upward and move to palm inward, facing the signer, with a flick of the wrist. The interpreter misses the novelty or importance of the information.

2d.   Numbering systems are interpreted inaccurately.

ASL has a rich system for expressing numbers. Often, however, because of the complexity of the numbering systems in ASL and interpreters' lack of comprehension abilities, errors occur in interpretation. For example, when the sign for FIRST-PLACE is used, the interpretation is "one." The audience may be told "an athlete got one medal," but the signer said, "he got a first place medal." Or, when the signer is expressing an age concept about someone who is in her THIRTIES, it is interpreted as either "three years old" or "thirty years old."

Sometimes the referent <u>and</u> the number are wrongly interpreted. For instance, the interpreter says, "second floor," when the signer conveys "third place." (See also Referencing.)

**2e. When number incorporation is used, the interpretation
is inaccurate.**

Number incorporation is often used in ASL. For example, the sign
THREE-DAY is a single sign composed of the sign DAY plus
THREE. In handling ASL number incorporation strategies,
interpreters often get the number component wrong. For instance, the
signer may say TWO-WEEK-AGO and the interpreter says, "three
weeks ago" because he or she misunderstood the number.

3. ASL lexicon (vocabulary) is interpreted accurately.

Possible errors

> 3a. The meaning of ASL signs is omitted: The interpreter
> substitutes the word "personnel" for the sign PERSONALITY.
> 3b. Possessive pronouns are confused with nominative pronouns:
> "His" is used instead of "he."
> 3c. Nouns are interpreted as verbs or verbs are interpreted as
> nouns: AIRPLANE is interpreted as "fly."
> 3d. When noun classifications are used, the interpretation is
> inaccurate: APPLE-ORANGE-BANANA is interpreted as
> individual lexical items rather than "fruit."
> 3e. When compound signs are used, the interpretation is
> inaccurate: TRUE͡WORK is interpreted as "really works" as
> opposed to "I'm not joking."
> 3f. Body-anchored signs are interpreted inaccurately:
> OPERATE-ON-WRIST is interpreted as just "operate."
> 3g. New or regional signs (e.g., INTERNET, E-MAIL) are
> interpreted inaccurately: INTERNET is signed and the
> interpreter says "networking."

Discussion

3a.   The meaning of ASL signs is omitted.

At times ASL signs are unfamiliar to interpreters and omissions of meaning result. (This problem is different from omissions of meaning caused by the interpretation process itself). Sometimes an unfamiliar sign is not noticed by an interpreter. For example, CONVINCE, signed with a quick two-handed chopping movement is missed. The interpreter says, "I talked to Joan and she will drive me home," when the signer's meaning is, "I talked to Joan and convinced her to drive me home."

3b.   Possessive pronouns are confused with nominative pronouns.

A relatively common occurrence in the research sample was confusion between the signs for possessive pronouns which use the whole hand (e.g., HIS, HERS, THEIRS) and nominative pronouns which use the index finger (e.g., HE, SHE, IT, THEY). HIS is a possessive pronoun and implies ownership. HE is a pronoun that has nothing to do with ownership; it "names" someone, the subject of an action. This slight difference in the pronoun interpretation greatly changes the meaning of the signer's message.

3c.   Nouns are interpreted as verbs or verbs are interpreted as nouns.

At times, nouns and verbs in ASL are rendered incorrectly in English. For example the signer meant, "I was <u>flying</u> in a holding pattern for one hour," and used the verb FLY to convey this. The interpreter conveys the verb FLY as a noun, "plane." As a result the target language message is, "The <u>plane</u> was in a holding pattern for one hour." The interpretation gives no information about whether or not the signer was in the plane, and equivalency is lost.

41

In ASL some nouns and verbs are signed in the same way – although signers may use non-manual markers or movement to differentiate meaning. For example, TO-GET-ANGRY and ANGER can be signed the same way. The interpreter must grasp verb/noun distinctions the signer intends and communicate these ideas in the correct English grammatical structure.

Also, nouns and verbs in ASL can be combined into one sign, for example WEAR-CLOTHES. Both the noun and the verb need to be represented in the target language, for instance, "the clothes I was wearing were new," and not, "The clothes were new." If only the noun or the verb is present in the target language, an incomplete message may be provided, unless the context of the message provides the audience with all required information.

3d.   When noun classifications are used, the interpretation is inaccurate.

ASL uses grouping nouns to convey a generic idea, for example APPLE-ORANGE-BANANA for "fruit." This feature of ASL is referred to as noun classification. When signers use noun classification in ASL, often the interpretation is more effective if the generic English word is used as opposed to identifying the signer's list of lexical items. For example, if the signer signs KNIFE-FORK-SPOON, the interpreter can name the individual signs or use the generic noun to which those particular signs refer, "silverware." In English the generic noun would normally be chosen to convey "silverware" and individual words "knife," "fork" and "spoon" would be used only to identify each item specifically. This might happen if someone is explaining where the fork, knife and spoon should go on a formal place setting or how one organizes them in a silverware drawer. In such cases the interpretation should retain the separate lexical labels of the "knife," "fork" and "spoon." Otherwise, it is a misinterpretation not to use a generic noun.

Sometimes, the generic noun does not necessarily mean each individual sign used in the utterance. For example, the noun classification of APPLE-ORANGE-BANANA conveys the meaning of "fruit." If the signer went shopping and bought "fruit," she did not necessarily buy apples, oranges and bananas; she might have purchased grapes, bananas and watermelon. The same is true for KNIFE-FORK-SPOON above.

When the signer uses noun classifications and the interpretation conveys each sign, this is often referred to as a-word-for-word translation or English glossing. Meaning is often skewed in this type of interpretation. For example, if individual lexical items are used, the audience will most likely be waiting to know why specificity was introduced in the text. When the reasons do not become evident in the interpretation, the result is a puzzled audience. If this is a pattern in the interpretation, the audience will experience a message less-than-equivalent to the signer's intent.

3e. When compound signs are used, the interpretation is inaccurate.

A compound sign consists of two individual signs that are combined to form a new sign with a different meaning. For example, TALK͡NAME represents "to talk about." If the two individual signs that formed the compound are conveyed separately in the interpretation, the meaning is skewed. The meaning of the individual signs, instead of the meaning of a compound, come through in the interpretation.

3f. Body-anchored signs are interpreted inaccurately.

Body-anchored signs are signs that point to or are placed at specific locations on the body, such as OPERATE-ON-FINGER. Interpretations must then include the location of the surgery and not just that surgery took place. For example, the sign ACHE-AT-STOMACH must include both of the elements "ache" or "pain" and "stomach." "Stomach ache" is an acceptable interpretation, but not just "ache" or just "stomach."

3g. New or regional signs (e.g., INTERNET, E-MAIL) are interpreted accurately.

Like all languages, ASL often has new lexical items introduced to it. For example, when a newly elected prime minister or president takes office, she or he is often in the news. Over time a name sign referring to these individuals may become common usage in ASL. Interpreters must keep abreast of these new lexical items and region-specific signs to ensure that they can provide complete and accurate interpretations for the audience. For example, the sign for the Edmonton Oilers hockey team – signed with an O-handshape circling on the chest – could be misinterpreted as "the team that had no numbers on their jerseys" if interpreters were not familiar with this region-specific sign.

NOTE: As in any language, regional variation is a significant part of communication. For example in ASL, people or places that are talked about frequently may have signs that are commonly recognized in one region, but not in others. These signs may be carried over to different regions where they are not well known by interpreters. The signer may, for instance, be signing about his place of employment in New York at the National Institute of the Deaf, N-T-I-D. This discussion may take place at a conference in Boston. Interpreters must be aware of topics that are frequently referred to, or are common in the area of deafness among deaf signers but may not be familiar to audiences in other regions, or non-deaf audiences.

4. Classifiers or Size and Shape Specifiers (SASS) are used accurately.

Possible errors

4a. The referent indicated by the classifier/SASS is interpreted inaccurately or omitted altogether: The interpreter says "truck" instead of "car."

4b. The movement depicted by the classifier/SASS is interpreted inaccurately: The interpretation is "walking up hill," but the signer meant "walking up a windy hill."

4c. When classifiers/SASS are used to describe the size or shape of specific objects, the interpretation is inaccurate: The interpreter conveys "a thin pole" instead of "a thick pole."

4d. When more than one classifier or SASS is used, their relationship is interpreted inaccurately: The interpretation is "The car hit a person," and should be, "The person ran into the car."

4e. The non-manual markers associated with classifiers and SASS are interpreted inaccurately: The interpreter says "extremely deep" for "shallow."

Discussion

Classifiers (CL) and size and shape specifiers (SASS) are often present in ASL and are used for a variety of functions. For example, they can be used as nouns or verbs, and as adjectives or adverbs. They are used to describe the sizes, shapes, locations and relationships of items.

In ASL the referent (e.g., #CAR or P-E-G-G-Y) is usually identified first and followed by the classifier and/or the SASS. "The car" or "Peggy" is identified first and then the classifier for "vehicle" or "person" can be used.

Classifiers may represent nouns, verbs, pronouns, or may modify adjectives or adverbs:

o noun-classifier (e.g., the classifier meaning "vehicle": CL: 3, palm left, fingers out, not up. This could be used for "car," "truck," or "motorcycle," but not for "airplane.")

o pronoun-classifier (e.g., the classifier referring to "two people standing": CL: 2, palm out, fingers up. This could be used for two people of any size, gender, race, or age, but not for two animals.)

o verb-classifier (e.g., the "two people standing" classifier, in the previous example, becomes a verb classifier for "two people walking" – the action verb is incorporated into the pronoun classifier if the "two-hand" moves forward.)

45

- o adjectival modifier (e.g., to show that the "two people standing" are thin, an adjectival modifier is added by using a non-manual marker – sucking in the cheeks.)
- o adverbial modifier (e.g., in conveying two drunken people standing unsteadily, the adverbial classifier is a rocking movement added to the "two people standing" pronoun classifier from the example above.)

4a. The referent indicated by the classifier/SASS is interpreted inaccurately or omitted altogether.

Sometimes referents are interpreted inaccurately. For example, if the signer talked about breaking her foot, F-O-O-T might be spelled followed by a classifier identifying the foot and how it was actually broken. A SASS could be used to express that the foot is swollen and bruised. If the signed message indicating the classifier referent (e.g., the broken foot) is misunderstood, the interpretation might end up wrongly referring to a hand.

4b. The movement depicted by the classifier/SASS is interpreted inaccurately.

Movement must be conveyed correctly when interpreting the signer's use of classifiers. For example, a speeding truck passing a slow moving car can be signed #CAR + CL: 3 vehicle-UP-HILL-SLOW (using the non-dominant hand), T-R-U-C-K + CL: 3 vehicle-UP-HILL-PASS (using the dominant hand). It would be wrong to interpret that the car passed the truck. SASS can be used to express other kinds of movement as well. They can show the movement of a spill or of a waterfall – for example FLOOR + WATER + SPREAD-LEFT, or MOUNTAIN + WATER + SPREAD-DOWN. It would be wrong to interpret the adverbial modifier SPREAD-LEFT as "the water on the left" without indicating the spilling action of the water.

4c. When classifiers/SASS are used to describe the size or shape of specific objects, the interpretation is inaccurate.

Description using classifiers and SASS can be conveyed in ASL by slight changes in the production of the sign, which can be missed by an interpreter. SASS can be used, for example, to describe the painted lines between cars in a parking lot. Are they faded? Are they thick or thin? Are they straight or crooked? Are they of different sizes, perhaps larger for the handicapped parking spaces? This might be important information.

When classifiers and SASS are used in ASL, they often require descriptive English terminology to render accurate interpretations. For example, when the signer talks about a table, the use of SASS will also convey that the table is round or oblong. Or, if signing about a swimming pool, the SASS may indicate the pool is kidney shaped or a lap pool. English adjectives often provide the necessary detail for the audience. Without the addition of these adjectives, the message is less colorful, less complete and less accurate.

4d. When more than one classifier or SASS is used, their relationship is interpreted inaccurately.

The interpretation is often less accurate when more than one classifier or SASS is used at the same time. When this happens, the interpreter may not only miss the referents of the classifiers, but also the relationships that the signer is expressing. For example, classifiers and SASS can be used by signers to describe the relationship of geographic places to each other. The relationship of British Columbia and Nova Scotia will typically be signed with B-C on the signer's left (i.e., west) and N-O-V-A S-C-O-T-I-A, in the east, on the signer's right. To describe flying in either direction, the interpretation should include the direction of the flight such as flying east from B.C. to Nova Scotia. Or, if the signer identifies Los Angeles and Florida using classifiers, the interpretation must make it clear which one is which, using knowledge of geography, and of classifiers and the use of space.

4e. The non-manual markers associated with classifiers and SASS are interpreted inaccurately.

The non-manual markers associated with classifiers and SASS add significant meaning to the message. Their meaning must be included in the interpretation. For example, if, when talking about a wire the signer uses the pursed lips non-manual marker, this can mean the wire is small or thin, or both. If the non-manual marker of pursed lips is overlooked or not interpreted, the message conveyed might be about a regular-sized wire, rather than the small and/or the thin one.

NOTE: There are occasions when it is not important to retain the degree of specificity the signer provides in the interpretation. At times, ASL may be more specific than English requires. For example, in ASL when describing how an accident occurred, the signer, due to the visual features of ASL, may be very exact about where his car hit another car. In English this information is sometimes conveyed in a general manner. For example, the interpreter might say, "I was in a fender bender that was my fault," rather than saying, "my car's right front bumper hit the other car's passenger door." Even though, all of this meaning is present in the signer's message, it would only be required in the target message if the specificity is significant in the context like making an insurance claim. Otherwise it is too specific and will sound peculiar in English.

5. Non-manual markers such as CHA, co-occurring with the sign BIG to express "huge," are interpreted accurately. (See also Referencing.)

Possible errors

5a. Facial adjectives are interpreted inaccurately: The meaning of the non-manual marker of PAH meaning "success" is interpreted as "careful."

5b. Facial adverbs are interpreted inaccurately: The meaning "careless" or "inattentive" expressed by the non-manual marker, TH, is omitted.

5c. Eye gaze is interpreted inaccurately: The significance of the signer looking at a particular space to indicate a referent is missed.

5d. Non-manual markers of the head and torso are interpreted inaccurately: A signer's headshake meaning "no" is omitted.

Discussion

Non-manual markers associated with ASL lexicon add meaning to a signed message. They include movements and positions of the eyes, mouth, face, head and torso. Non-manual markers can be used as adjectives or adverbs and used simultaneously with signs. For example, the sign FAR takes the additional meaning of "very far" when an eye squint is used the head moves slightly backwards.

Some non-manual markers can actually change the meaning of signs so that the non-manual marker/sign combination must be interpreted in a completely different way than the sign produced without the marker. For example, one of the differences between NOT-YET and LATE, is that NOT-YET has the tongue slightly showing. In this instance, the non-manual marker of the tongue does not <u>add</u> meaning to the sign, but completely alters it.

5a.   Facial adjectives are interpreted inaccurately.

Facial adjectives are as important as the signs they accompany and need to have their meaning expressed in the English interpretation. For example, if the signer is talking about "boxes" and uses slit eyes and a tight mouth, she or he may mean "a large number of boxes." Teeth showing can mean "many" or "huge." A whistling mouth that is sucking in can mean "few" or "not far." When these meanings are omitted or misunderstood, errors are present in the interpretation.

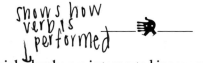

shows how verb is performed

5b. **Facial adverbs are interpreted inaccurately.**

The facial adverb, TH, with the tongue slightly exposed can add the adverbial "something different from the norm," or "out of alignment," perhaps referring to the way a car is parked on the street or in a parking lot. The exact meaning depends on the context, the signer's eye gaze and the precise manner in which the TH non-manual is formed.

5c. **Eye gaze is interpreted inaccurately.**

Eye gaze often indicates to whom or to what the signer is referring and the relationship between the topics discussed. These details can be lost in the interpretation. Eye gaze is also used to convey specificity. If, for example, the signer conveys "that chair in particular" with eye gaze and the interpreter misses the specificity of the reference, equivalency will be lost.

NOTE: Often in ASL, eye gaze is used to single out individuals. For example, the signer says THANK YOU with eye gaze at Hans. In this case saying, "Thank you, Hans," captures the meaning of the eye gaze.

5d. **Non-manual markers of the head and torso are interpreted inaccurately.**

Non-manual markers using the head and torso can indicate meanings such as negation, tense and emphasis. When negation is expressed, the head can move from left to right simultaneously with a sign like WANT or HAVE, changing the meaning to "don't want" and "don't have." The head and torso will move slightly backward to indicate past tense or slightly forward to indicate future tense. The interpreter may not notice these subtle movements and neglect to alter the tense. To express emphasis the signer's head and shoulders may closely support the direction of the signing. For example, the signer means "I looked high and low for that book – using LOOK-FOR and following the sign intently with head movement. The interpreter only conveys "I looked for it" because the head movement was not noticed.

6. Negation is accurately conveyed in English.

Possible errors

6a. Negation is omitted: "Want" is conveyed instead of "<u>don't</u> want."

6b. Negation is incorrectly attached to utterances: When negation is placed at the end of the first phrase such as ME CAR OWN NOT, PREFER WALK, meaning, "I don't own a car because I prefer to walk" the interpreter says, "I own a car because I don't like to walk."

6c. Negation is added when it is not in the source message.

Discussion

ASL conveys negation in several different ways:

o by reversing the sign itself (e.g., DON'T-KNOW, DON'T-WANT);

o by using a negating sign (e.g., NEVER, NOT) within the utterance, before the sign or idea to be negated or at the end of the utterance;

o by shaking one's head "no" while signing; and,

o by placing the negation at the end of the sentence or repeating negation at the end of sentences when negation is emphasized or is the point.

6a. Negation is omitted.

Omissions in interpretations were more evident in the research material when a non-manual negation behavior was used without a negative sign. For example, I ENJOY READ accompanied with a shake of the head throughout the utterance meaning "not" or a facial expression displaying dislike or negation can be misinterpreted as, "I enjoy reading very much."

6b. Negation is incorrectly attached to utterances.

Negation is often signed at the end of sentences. Care must be taken in the interpretation so that the negation is not attributed to following sentences. For example, the ASL sentence ME LIKE APPLES NOT, BUT ME LIKE BANANAS can be misinterpreted as, "I like apples, but I don't like bananas." It should be, "I don't like apples, but I like bananas." This type of error in which negation is attached to a subsequent sentence or phrase and not the one to which it belongs was common in the research sample.

6c. Negation is added when it is not in the source message.

Sometimes negation is added in the interpretation when this is not the signer's intent. For example, MY HOUSE BIG can be misinterpreted as "My house is not big." The signing emphasis in this case is misread as negation.

7. When emphasis is used, it is interpreted accurately.

Possible errors

7a. When signs are modulated to incorporate emphasis, the interpretation is inaccurate: The signer inflects the sign for SLOW to mean "extremely slow" and the interpretation is "not very slow" or "quickly."

7b. Rhetorical questions used for emphasis in ASL are interpreted inaccurately: The signer says, "Where did I just come from? New York." and the interpreter says, "I'm from New York."

7c. When eye gaze is used for emphasis, it is interpreted inaccurately: The signer purposefully looks away from the truck, meaning she is not watching the truck and the interpreter says, "I was watching the truck."

7d. When fingerspelling or signs are used for emphasis, they are interpreted inaccurately: The interpreter makes no distinction between the emphatic signing or spelling and the rest of the message.

7e. Emphatic repetition is interpreted inaccurately: The signer repeats LIKE to mean he "really likes one thing" and the interpreter says, "likes everything."

7f. When bracketing of information is used for emphasis, it is interpreted into inaccurate English: ME HATE READ BOOK, HATE is interpreted "I hate reading books, hate it," instead of "I really hate reading books."

Discussion

7a.   When signs are modulated to incorporate emphasis, the interpretation is inaccurate.

Signs can be modulated or inflected to reflect emphasis. When signs are formed more slowly than usual in combination with an intense eye gaze, then emphasis is likely present in the source message. For example, if the signer indicated that the door shut and modulated the sign CLOSE-DOOR, then the interpretation must include the meaning "slammed shut."

7b.   Rhetorical questions used for emphasis in ASL are interpreted inaccurately.

Since rhetorical questions are primarily used for emphasis in ASL, the point that is being made must be appropriately emphatic in the interpretation. Often retaining the ASL rhetorical form in the English interpretation is ineffective. The question structure does not reflect the same emphasis in English as it does in ASL. In the example, ME WORK SATURDAY SUNDAY WHY, EARN-MONEY NEED it is more effective in English to say, "I am working this Saturday and Sunday because I need the money," than to say, "Why am I working this Saturday and Sunday? It is because I need the money." (See also Intrusions.)

7c.   When eye gaze is used for emphasis, it is interpreted inaccurately.

Another way that ASL marks emphasis is through the use of eye gaze. If eye gaze is directed at a specific location along with a sign or a fingerspelled word the message is emphatic. For example, when eye gaze is used in connection with a classifier of a parked car and is directed at the sign, it means that specific car in that specific spot, not just any car. When there is a lack of specific eye gaze, it usually implies that the point is not significant. It is important to note that eye gaze can also be used specifically to indicate the opposite of emphatic attention. The signer can use eye gaze to express inattentiveness or ignoring by purposefully glancing away.

7d.   When fingerspelling or signs are used for emphasis, they are interpreted inaccurately.

Fingerspelling is another way that emphasis is conveyed in ASL. For example, if a person really hates to fly, he may choose to spell F-L-Y for emphasis, rather than using a sign. If fingerspelling is produced at a slower rate (i.e., modulated), and/or delivered in a staccato manner, or if the eye gaze is directed toward the fingerspelling, then emphasis is probably intended and this emphasis must be conveyed in the interpretation.

Using particular signs such as THAT or THAT-ONE can also convey emphasis. For example, ME SAW THAT BOY, indicates that it is a particular boy, perhaps the same boy that I saw at the baseball game last night. It is not simply "a boy." The interpretation must be equally emphatic and specific.

7e. Emphatic repetition is interpreted inaccurately.

Repetition of signs conveys emphasis. For example, if an experienced real estate agent who has no knowledge of cars, finds herself buying a new car, she might sign ME BUY HOUSE CAN, C-A-R CAN'T, CAN'T. This can be interpreted as, "I can buy a house without any problems, but I can't possibly buy a car!" If the emphasis is missing, then it can be inaccurately interpreted as, "I can buy a house, but I can't buy a car." In this instance, the information is present, but the emphasis is missing and therefore the interpretation is not equivalent.

7f. When bracketing of information is used for emphasis, it is interpreted inaccurately into English.

Another repetition strategy used to convey emphasis is to use bracketing, or reiterate information by using the same lexical item or items at the beginning and end of an utterance. For example, NEW GLASSES, ME BUY, NEW, would be wrongly interpreted as "I bought new glasses" when the ASL message conveyed "I bought brand new glasses!"

Emphasis can also be conveyed by repeating the use of the question mark sign at the beginning and the end of an utterance – QUESTION, YOU PREGNANT, QUESTION. It is most often used to emphasize that an important question is about to be asked. It is not commonly used as a punctuation mark at the end of every question. Regular usage of question marks is often seen among novice, non-deaf signers. (See also Intrusions.)

55

8. When signs are modulated (i.e., inflected) the interpretation is accurate.

Possible errors

8a. When verbs are modulated, they are interpreted inaccurately: The sign for LOOK, with amazement, is interpreted as "glance at."

8b. When nouns are modulated, they are interpreted inaccurately: The sign for HOUSE, signed using a great deal of space, is interpreted as "house" instead of "the very large house."

8c. When pronouns are modulated, they are interpreted inaccurately: MINE, signed strongly, is interpreted without emphasis.

8d. When non-manual markers are used to modulate the meaning of signs, they are interpreted inaccurately: The sign SMALL is used with squinting eyes and pursed lips, but the interpretation is "small" instead of "very small" or "miniscule."

8e. When singular and/or plural forms are used, the interpretation is inaccurate: The signer means "brother," but the interpreter says, "brothers."

Discussion

Modulation or inflection, as it is also called, is a crucial component of ASL. It appears in many different forms. For example, changing the direction in which a verb is produced can affect the meaning greatly as in LOOK-LEFT, or LOOK-RIGHT. This is also true for the sign LOOK alone. If the sign is inflected by the addition of non-manual markers, LOOK, can mean "look with shock" or "look with disgust."

8a.   When verbs are modulated, they are interpreted inaccurately.

Interpreters tend to retain the meaning of a verb, but miss the inflection altogether. For example, the signer uses WANT with wiggling fingers, and the interpreter says, "I want it," instead of conveying the meaning, "I can't live without it."

8b.   When nouns are modulated, they are interpreted inaccurately.

Modulation of nouns can show intensity, size, shape and the quality of objects as well as spatial arrangements. For example, the sign PERSON can be modulated to show size by placing the hands relatively close to one another, meaning a very slim individual, or it can refer to a certain spatial location by positioning the sign to the left or to the right of the signer. The interpreter may miss this positioning and leave out "the person over on the right" or "on the left."

8c.   When pronouns are modulated, they are interpreted inaccurately.

Pronouns, such as THEIR, YOUR and WE can be modulated, or inflected to indicate the specific person or group of persons to which the signer is referring. For example, the sign for HE can point to the man on the left, or on the right. The sign YOUR can indicate that something belongs to one person, but by moving the sign in an arc, it means belonging to more than one individual, "all of your."

Classifiers can work as pronouns and can be modulated to include information about what the person represented is doing or what is happening to them, thus including the action of a verb with the classifier. For example, a classifier used for a person standing (e.g., CL-INDEX) can be modulated to include a verb such as "a person standing and walking backwards" (e.g., CL-INDEX moving backwards). When classifiers are modulated, the additional meaning that the modulation conveys must be incorporated into the interpretation.

8d.   When non-manual markers are used to modulate the meaning of signs, they are interpreted inaccurately.

Signs can be modulated by using non-manual markers as well. For example, by changing a non-manual marker, negation can be conveyed. If the head moves from left to right it negates the entire sentence. If this subtle modulation is overlooked, the interpretation will inaccurately convey the signer's message in the affirmative. Non-manuals can also be added to adverbial phrases and are easily missed. For example, to indicate an action "in the future," WILL can be signed to convey "in the distant future." The sign WILL can be signed with the co-occurring non-manual of puffed cheeks to convey the additional meaning of "a long time" in the future.

8e.   When singular and/or plural forms are used, the interpretation is inaccurate.

It is important to identify whether one or more persons or things is referred to in an utterance. At times the singular or plural form in the interpretation does not affect the meaning of the message, whereas other times it impacts the message greatly. For example, the sign PERSON can be modulated to refer to several persons by repeating the sign in different locations. If the signer places a classifier in several locations CL: 3 "vehicle" (on left+++), he or she means that there are several cars parked on the left. The interpretation, "the car on the left," would be inaccurate.

9. The temporal aspects of the message are interpreted accurately and convey the signer's perspective on events.

Possible errors

9a. Verb tense is interpreted inaccurately: The signer says, "I've done it," and the interpreter says, "I will do it."

9b. Duration is interpreted inaccurately: The signer means, "I worked on it for ages," and the interpreter says, "I worked very hard."

9c. Intensity is interpreted inaccurately: The interpretation is "She had her baby," instead of "The baby was just born!"

9d. Frequency is interpreted inaccurately: "Quickly" is substituted for "often."

Discussion

In ASL, verbs are modulated to provide temporal information. Temporal aspect refers to the inclusion of time-related meaning in an utterance. For example, modulation indicates whether something was done quickly in a short period of time or done gradually over a long period of time. To indicate future tense, signs such as WILL, NEXT-YEAR, or TOMORROW can be added to the verb, while adding FINISH or PAST indicates the action is completed.

Alternatively, ASL verbs can be modulated with co-occurring non-manual markers and/or by altering the sign movement. For example, by using non-manual markers with the verb WORK, the phrases "working hard" and "working for a long time" are differentiated. Non-manuals can provide very specific information. These signs function like adverbs in English, which are added to provide information about how an action occurs. For example English might require the addition of an adverb or adverb phrase like "hard" or "for a long time" to qualify the verb "laugh." In ASL the sign LAUGH would be modulated in a particular way for each meaning.

9a.   Verb tense is interpreted inaccurately.

If a verb is unmarked in ASL, it is considered present tense. Once time has been established, everything that follows is in the same tense until a change in tense is explicitly stated. When a different time is required, the signer will indicate the change with lexical or non-manual markers. Interpreters find it relatively easy to interpret temporal aspects of the signer's message when added adverbial signs are used – such as NEXT-WEEK. However, they tend to have more trouble when time is indicated by the use of co-occurring non-manual markers and/or by movement added to the sign. If for instance, the non-manual marker CS meaning "recently" co-occurring with the verb is missed, the newly articulated time, the changed time, may not be interpreted accurately. The tense in the interpretation may wrongly be that of the previous information. Or, if the non-manual marker of shifting slightly forward meaning "later" or "in the future" is missed, the interpretation may wrongly continue in the present tense.

9b.   Duration is interpreted inaccurately.

Signs can be repeated with certain movements along with appropriate non-manuals to convey various kinds of temporal information, such as duration (i.e., for how long an action occurred). For example, the signer alters the way PAINT is signed and says LAST-WEEK, HOUSE PAINT along with the non-manual puffed cheeks to convey that he worked on painting his house all last week. The interpreter missing the change in movement and the non-manual might say, "I've finished painting the house last week."

9c.   Intensity is interpreted inaccurately.

The modulation of signs is also changed to express intensity or the signer's feelings about an action. For instance, the sign WORK can be repeated in a labored manner to indicate hard or arduous activity.

9d.   Frequency is interpreted inaccurately.

Frequency, or how often something happens, is also conveyed by modulations. The signer might indicate that he gets the flu often by spelling F-L-U and moving the sign for SICK in an arc more than once. If an interpreter misses the modulated sign, he or she may incorrectly say, "I got the flu."

10. **Distribution of an action conveyed by inflected verbs is interpreted accurately.**

Possible errors

10a. Distinctions between the involvement of some, many or all of the people, places or things are inaccurate: The signer means, "I have visited all fifty states," and the interpretation is, "I've visited several states."

10b. Distinctions between ALL and EACH are inaccurate: "I passed out flyers to the class," is signed and the interpreter says, "I passed out flyers to each student."

Discussion

Some ASL verbs convey the distribution of an action. The interpretation should clearly reflect whether one or more than one person, place or thing is involved. If it is determined that more than one is involved, it must be made clear whether it was some, many or all. If all of the people, places or things are involved, the audience must know if each of them is involved individually or all are involved as a group.

10a. **Distinctions between the involvement of some, many or all of the people, places or things are inaccurate.**

Interpreters sometimes fail to convey distribution accurately. For example, a group is forming, and it is the signer's intent to describe the group as a whole entity. The interpreter, however, conveys a message about the individual participants in the group. This may seem like a minor detail, but the difference between these ideas will drastically change the signer's message.

10b.   Distinctions between ALL and EACH are inaccurate.

When distributional verbs (e.g., give) are used, information about how people, places, or things are involved is conveyed by specifying the manner of distribution. For example, the manner in which some papers were given out to the class of students can be an important piece of information to retain in the interpretation. Was the stack of papers given to one student? Did the teacher hand out the papers to a few specific students? Did he pass papers out to all of the students individually? In conveying this information in the target message, it would be important to distinguish between GIVE-ALL-TO-ONE, GIVE-TO-SPECIFIC-FEW, or GIVE-TO-EACH.

NOTE: There are occasions when it is not important to retain the degree of specificity the signer provides in the interpretation. At times, ASL may be more specific than English requires. For example, if the signer explains how all the birds dispersed in one direction, the sign for SCATTER will also include the direction the birds went, for instance to the left or to the west. This additional meaning is automatically present in the signing. It would only be required in the English interpretation if the direction they scattered is significant in the context. Otherwise it is too specific and will sound peculiar in English.

11.   When signed vocabulary is borrowed from English, or other signed languages (e.g., Australian Sign Language) or other signed systems (e.g., signed English), the interpretation is accurate.

Possible errors

11a. Initialized signs are interpreted inaccurately:
    REHABILITATION signed as HELP with an R, is
    interpreted as "reinforce."

11b. English affixes (e.g., bi-, -ing, -ment) are interpreted inaccurately: B-I + LANGUAGE is interpreted as "language" instead of "bilingual."

11c. Borrowed signs from other countries are interpreted inaccurately: Japanese signers use 'g' handshapes (fingers of left and right hand touching each other, then moving away to index and thumb touching) to indicate their country. The interpreter who only knows the ASL sign for Japan, misreads the indigenous sign as meaning "ashtray."

11d. Contact variety signing (i.e., code switching, sometimes referred to as PSE) is interpreted inaccurately: An ASL signer signs an English idiom SAME-AS, WATER O-F-F DUCK #BACK instead of the expected ASL sign equivalent, NOT-CARE. The interpreter doesn't catch the use of the English idiom and says, "like water flowing."

Discussion

English speakers borrow words from several languages such as French (e.g., déjà vu) and Spanish (e.g., patio). ASL also borrows from other languages such as English and other signed languages. Signers may fingerspell English words, add endings such as −ing, or use infinitives such as "to" as in ME WANT TO KNOW.

11a.   Initialized signs are interpreted inaccurately.

Initialized signs are not standardized and many interpreters are unfamiliar with these signs. For example, signs for "jam" and "just" both build off the letter "j" and produce the sign in the palm of the non-dominant hand. The interpreter must depend on context and knowledge of these particular initialized signs to produce a correct interpretation.

11b.   English affixes (e.g., bi-, -ing, -ment) are interpreted inaccurately.

English affixes are occasionally integrated into ASL signing. For example, a signer may use DEVELOP + -MENT or U-N + FRIENDLY. This non-standard ASL usage may be confusing to interpreters. In these examples, the target language message might come out as "deteriorating development" or "friendly."

11c.   Borrowed signs from other countries are interpreted inaccurately.

ASL borrows from other signed languages. Signers may integrate country signs that are used locally in foreign countries rather than using the ASL signs for countries that are commonly used in Canada and the United States. For example, ASL signs the word "China" by slightly twisting the index finger at the outside corner of the eye. However, the sign that many Chinese people in China use is an index finger touching the non-dominant shoulder, then moving to the dominant shoulder and down to the dominant waist near the hip. Interpreters may fail to recognize these borrowed signs.

11d.   Contact variety signing (i.e., code switching, sometimes referred to as PSE) is interpreted inaccurately.

Occasionally, when signs and/or meaning are borrowed from English, signers will alter the sequence of the signs. For example, signers might express the idea of "deafness" and sign "-NESS + DEAF" rather than "DEAF + -NESS." The signing of the English idiom "down to earth" might be signed "EARTH + DOWN." The signer might sign "PAINT + B-A-R-N + RED" for the English idiom "paint the town red." If the order of signing is different from English word order, or if the exact English idiom is not conveyed in the signed rendition, the interpretation will be skewed. To render an acceptable and equivalent interpretation in these instances, interpreters must comprehend the signed message <u>and</u> retrieve the English phrase or idiom that is most commonly expressed by native English speakers in a similar setting.

Comprehension:
ASL Discourse

OVERVIEW

Successful ASL comprehension involves more than the lexical knowledge discussed in the last section. Interpreters must also understand syntactic and idiomatic elements of ASL to provide equivalent interpretations.

An interpreter can get all the signs right and yet completely miss the signer's intent. Effective interpretation requires a sense of meaning conveyed not only by word choice, but also by phrases, sentences, paragraphs and the entire text. ASL discourse comprehension refers to the ability to grasp and convey this "big picture" meaning.

12. **ASL grammatical facial markers produced "above the nose" are interpreted accurately.**

Possible errors

12a. WH-questions like "who?" "what?" and "when?" are interpreted inaccurately: They are interpreted as negative emotions instead of questions.

12b. Yes-no questions, questions that can be answered with a "yes" or "no," are interpreted inaccurately: The signer says WE-TWO GO with raised eyebrows throughout the signing and the interpreter says, "You and I will go," instead of the question, "Are we going?"

12c. Statements are interpreted as questions: The signer says J-E-N-I SICK, NOW HEALTHY with eyebrows up on the first phrase and then lowered to mean, "Jeni was sick, but she's better now." The interpreter says, "Is Jeni sick or healthy?"

12d. The signer's emotions are confused with grammar: Anger is interpreted as a WH-question.

69

Discussion

ASL signers use facial markers to convey questions and emotions, among other things. Facial markers are also used in topicalization. Topicalization in ASL is similar to English speakers modulating their voice to attract the attention of the audience to the beginning of new sentences or to highlight an important part of a sentence.

12a.   WH-questions like "who?" "what?" and "when?" are interpreted inaccurately.

Often when questions are signed, the only clues indicating that a question is being asked are co-occurring non-manual markers above the nose. For WH-questions, those that begin with "where?" "when?" "why?" "what?" and "how?" the eyebrows tend to go down and create a small furrow. Interpreters occasionally perceive this questioning face as an unpleasant emotion and use declarative statement structures as opposed to question structures. For example, the question of WHEN LEAVE WORK combined with lower eyebrows might be misinterpreted as "I don't think you should be leaving work." The furrowed brow is interpreted as displeasure instead of as a question, and the interpretation is inaccurate.

12b.   Yes-no questions, questions that can be answered with a "yes" or "no," are interpreted inaccurately.

Yes-no questions are articulated in ASL with the eyebrows up. Examples of yes-no questions are, "Did you throw this morning's newspaper away?" or "Do you need a long vacation?" Occasionally, this facial marker is misinterpreted as indicating the topic of the sentence or as the beginning of a new paragraph. For instance, the interpreter omits the questions and says, "I threw the morning newspaper away," or "I need a long vacation."

12c.   Statements are interpreted as questions.

A complementary error also occurred frequently in the research samples. Inaccurate interpretation of topicalization in ASL, achieved by raising the eyebrows, was common. Declarative comments introducing new ideas were interpreted inaccurately as questions. For example, the statement TODAY #T-V V-I-O-L-E-N-T meaning, "These days programs on television are extremely violent," was misinterpreted as, "Is television violent these days?" The topicalization of TODAY with the use of raised eyebrows was interpreted inaccurately as a question.

12d.   The signer's emotions are confused with grammar.

Emotional overtones in the signer's message, like feelings of anger, were often misinterpreted in the research samples as WH-questions. For example, the statement ME MAD YOU meaning "I am very angry with you," can be misinterpreted as "Why are you so mad at me?"

The signer's emotions should not be confused with grammatical markers. If this mistake occurs a non-manual marker conveying anger or disappointment can be misinterpreted as a neutral statement or question and the emotional content of the message is lost.

13. ASL referencing is interpreted accurately.

Possible errors

13a. The subject talking or performing an action on someone or something is interpreted inaccurately: In the ASL sign ME-NOTICE, the subject is implied with the verb. The interpretation attributes the "noticing" to an individual other than the signer.

13b. The recipient of an action is not accurately identified in the interpretation: The signer says MY BOOK, ME-GIVE C-H-A-R-L-I-E and the interpretation is, "Charlie gave me a book." 71

13c. When nouns or concepts are established in space and referred to later, the interpretation is inaccurate:
The interpreter forgets where a signer has "placed" a noun.

13d. When space is restructured, it is interpreted inaccurately: The signer's perspective changes. Getting hit in the eye might first be signed to convey the person doing the hitting, then the person receiving the hit. In the target language message, the person who received the blow to the eye is inaccurate.

Discussion

ASL uses referencing to convey meaning related to the interactions of people, places and things. Often the cues used in ASL are subtle and can be missed in the interpretation.

ASL referencing is accomplished in several different ways:

o   ASL uses eye gaze to provide information about the person or thing being talked about. The direction of the signer's eye gaze provides important information about the topics, which the gaze highlights.

o   Orientation of the body, including the torso, the shoulders and the head, provides additional meaning to the message. This type of referencing is larger and therefore easier to notice than eye gaze. When body orientation is used with shifts in eye gaze, it can provide additional clues for identifying the referent.

o   Pointing or "indexing" is another common way to establish referents.

o   Characterization, taking on characters to relay an incident, is also a form of referencing in ASL. It includes movement of the head and eyes, pointing, body shifting, or any combination of these. Often, information about who is talking to whom is conveyed by the direction in which the signer is facing and the direction the signer is looking. At times, the direction the signer is looking is enough to convey this meaning and the orientation of the body and head remain constant.

o   A change in <u>style</u> of signing can be used to depict a character different from the signer, such as an old woman, or young child. This is signaled by changes in the physical stance of the signer. For example, when the signer describes an old woman and conveys what she said to the young child, the shoulders of the signer's body might become rounded and the torso lean

Comprehension: ASL Discourse

forward. The eyes might shift downward toward the child. When depicting the young child, the eyes might look up and the shoulders become straightened with the torso slightly leaning back. Also in referencing a young child, characterization may be conveyed by using less space and smaller signs, to depict an individual smaller than the signer.

o   The body itself can move in relation to the referent, to convey "towards," "away from" or "under."

It is important that both the subject and the object are identified in the interpretation every time they are required to make the message clear. It is a common error to omit information when referencing is used in ASL.

13a.   The subject talking or performing an action on someone or something is interpreted inaccurately.

A consistent problem for interpreters showed up in the research samples when the signer communicated directly with the audience and also used referencing and/or took on characters. At times when the signer is speaking directly to the audience, the interpretation conveys that a character is talking. For example, the signer is discussing her friend's opinion, then addresses the audience saying WHAT YOU THINK? The interpretation is "He asked me what I thought." The interpreter does not grasp who is asking the question. The "me" in the target language message suggests the signer is being asked the question, whereas the signer is addressing a question to the audience.

13b.   The recipient of an action is not accurately identified in the interpretation.

Often the interpretation is confused when the signer is telling a story that involves other people. Characters in the signer's account are not separated clearly and the identities of the "actors" and recipients of actions in the story become confused. For example, the signer says ME BUY TICKET FOR WIFE, ME. The interpreter gets the recipient wrong and says, "My wife bought me a ticket." The interpreter must get into the minds of the signers and see how he or she sees or saw an event, and voice it accordingly.

13c. **When nouns or concepts are established in space and referred to later, the interpretation is inaccurate.**

Interpreting can be faulty when the signer establishes nouns or concepts in space but those reference locations are overlooked or forgotten by the interpreter. For example TWIN F-R-A-T-E-R-N-A-L may be signed on the right, and TWIN I-D-E-N-T-I-C-A-L signed on the left, so they can be referred to later in the discourse. If the interpreter forgets which kind of twin is on the left, the referents in the interpretation will be confused.

13d. **When space is restructured, it is interpreted inaccurately.**

When space is restructured, messages are often misinterpreted. For example, a signer may discuss buying versus renting a house. She sets up HOUSE BUY on the right side of her signing space, and sets up HOUSE RENT on the left side of her signing space. After discussing these two topics, she then discusses the pros and cons of owning versus renting using these two "spaces." Later, she talks about only buying a house, and uses the same two spaces to convey the pros and cons of such a purchase. In other words she alters the meaning of the space by restructuring it. It is important for the interpreter to comprehend the initial use of space, and be alert to restructuring of that space by the signer.

Referencing is also used when describing something that will be done or was done by taking on the character(s) and actually demonstrating what was just described. The signer is communicating a change in perspective when he or she changes characters by restructuring space. After the perspective changes, to indicate a new character is speaking, the signer begins using characterization for referencing. For example, when talking about a fight, the signer says TWO MEN STANDING (facing each other) MAN-ON-LEFT-HIT-MAN-ON-RIGHT (FIST moving in neutral space from left to right). The signer then <u>becomes</u> the man on the right and signs FIST-IN-LEFT-EYE. This part of the signer's message is from a changed perspective – the signer is actually taking on the character of the man who receives a fist in the left eye. The interpretation needs to include not only that it was the man on the left who hit the man on the right, but also that the man on the right was hit in the eye. The signer conveys this by becoming the recipient of the action and showing that his left eye got hit. If this ASL referencing strategy is missed, the interpreter may leave out the information that the blow was delivered to the eye.

14. **Spatial relationships are interpreted accurately. (See also Referencing.)**

Possible errors

14a. When spatial relationships are established, the interpretation is inaccurate: The signer indicated his car was parked on the left side of the bus and the interpretation is the vehicles were one behind the other.

14b. When spatial relationships are changed, the interpretation is inaccurate: A book is "moved" from the chair to a table and the interpretation still refers to the book on the chair.

14c. An interpretation is inaccurate when the signer uses spatial location to identify a particular referent throughout his or her discourse: The city is introduced in the beginning of the text and established in space, for example M-I-L-A-N THERE. Later in the text, the spatial referent, THERE, is used alone. The interpretation does not refer to "Milan," although the English audience needs this spoken reference point.

14d. When the non-dominant hand is used to express spatial relationships, the interpretation is inaccurate: When the right-handed signer lists her siblings with her left hand, the relationship of the siblings is omitted.

14e. When different perspectives are signed, the interpretation is inaccurate: In a story about a couple, the wife's and the husband's perspectives are both interpreted as the wife's.

Discussion

ASL uses the space above the head, in front of the body and to the sides of the body. Space behind the signer is also used, but much less frequently than the space in front of the signer. The body and face will support the way space is used.

Spatial relationships are communicated in ASL using the same techniques that are used to reference particular objects. Directional verbs, eye gaze, role shifts and the location where a sign is produced all use space meaningfully.

14a.   When spatial relationships are established, the interpretation is inaccurate.

If the manner in which signs are produced indicates a relationship between the topics the signer is talking about, this relationship must be conveyed in the interpretation. For example, if something is far in the distance, the signing of verbs such as FAR, might be lofted in an arc-like movement rather than simply moving in a straight line. The eyes will probably also squint to emphasize distance. In these ways the signer is conveying his/her physical separation from a geographic point some distance away.

A signer may convey the relationship among various topics and subtopics by indexing, pointing with the index finger. The interpreter must grasp this element of ASL discourse. Indexing can refer to a certain topic, or it can refer to all of the topics presented depending on how the sign is used in space. For example, the signer may use space to compare the traveling time required for different kinds of boats – sailboats, powerboats and yachts. The sailboat's speed can be ranked against the other two boats in the group or it can be compared to either the yacht or the powerboat. This element of comparison must be present in the interpretation.

14b. **When spatial relationships are changed, the interpretation is inaccurate.**

The signer may change his or her use of space as the discourse progresses. For example, a signer might talk about BONITA (left) and SAM (right), MEET (center or neutral space). Later, they are married and the signer will place both of them on the right side of the signing space and refer to THOSE-TWO. So, the spatial relationship has been changed. The signer now refers to THEM as a couple as opposed to two individuals who just met. It is crucial that the interpretation also convey the change in relationship between Bonita and Sam by accurately interpreting the signer's use of space.

14c. **An interpretation is inaccurate when the signer uses spatial location to identify a particular referent throughout his or her discourse.**

Distant cohesion refers to the communication strategy of "coming back" to a previously discussed point. The signer may talk about something and set it up in space such as in DUCK OUTSIDE POINT-LEFT. If the signer doesn't use that particular space again the duck is still "held" in that location even though it is not mentioned. The signer may then refer to the duck much later by pointing to the duck's space. Interpreters are required to remember what is held where.

Distant cohesion may be used many times by a signer throughout a discourse. When more than one referent is held in space for later reference, it requires skill on the part of the interpreter to retain the "held" spaces for future use in the interpretation. These spaces may be held for a series of names such as two couples: Barb and Kelly, Maria and Muhammad. The interpreter must not only remember these names, but also their relationships to each other and to the signer.

14d.   When the non-dominant hand is used to express spatial relationships, the interpretation is inaccurate.

During the discourse, signers may use the non-dominant hand to convey meaning about relationships. The use of the non-dominant hand may occur independently, or both hands may be used simultaneously. Relational information relayed by both hands must be retained in the interpretation. For example, the non-dominant hand may be used to indicate the birth order of five siblings in a family. When referring to the youngest child who died ten years ago, the pinky finger of the non-dominant hand might be bent into the palm, and the relationship of this child to the other children must be stated in the interpretation. Simply interpreting that "a child died," or "one of the children in the family died," is insufficient if the signer is saying that it was the youngest sibling in the family who died.

14e.   When different perspectives are signed, the interpretation is inaccurate.

Often signers structure space to present different perspectives on the same event. The interpretation must incorporate all the perspectives mentioned in the source message. For example, a signer might talk about visiting a famous actor, Denzel Washington, and going to his home. When the signer first mentions the home it is in the distance. Then the perspective changes as he approaches the front door and walks into the house. Another example would be if a signer changes perspective while describing remodeling of kitchen cupboards. The signer might talk about the cupboards and also talk about what goes into the cupboards such as the glasses, plates and bowls. Or, he or she might move back and forth to convey the appearance of the outside and inside of the cupboard. The signer's perspective changes from the large view of all the kitchen cupboards to the smaller view of individual cupboards. The interpreter must follow the signing journey.

15. Utterance boundaries, delineating units of thought, are interpreted accurately.

Possible errors

15a. When a lexical item is used for an utterance boundary, it is interpreted inaccurately: UNDERSTAND++ meaning "but" is interpreted as, "Do you understand?"

15b. When a pause is used for the utterance boundary, it is interpreted inaccurately: The pause is missed and the interpreter produces a run-on sentence in the target language.

15c. When an eye blink or head nod is used for the utterance boundary, it is interpreted inaccurately: The signer says ME GO-TO WORK HATE (blink) #BUSY. The interpreter says, "I am going to work; I hate to be busy" instead of "I hate to go to work. It's so busy."

15d. When a shift in the physical stance of the body is made for the utterance boundary, it is interpreted inaccurately: The signer makes an utterance boundary by shifting the body weight to indicate a future action, but the interpreter reads the change as the introduction of a new character.

15e. When the signer's hands are used for the utterance boundary, it is interpreted inaccurately: The signer's hands and arms are slightly lowered for a pause, but the interpretation comes to a complete halt.

15f. When a new topic is introduced, the interpretation is inaccurate: New information is incorrectly applied to the previous topic.

Discussion

Utterance boundaries define units of thought in ASL. They are the way in which information is organized and provided to the audience, performing a function like punctuation in English. Utterance boundaries are a specific kind of discourse marker that conveys various transitions in the signer's message. They are used to structure discourse in a clear manner for the audience by highlighting the beginnings and ends of sections. They are also used by signers to introduce characterization, perhaps with eye gaze or body shift. It is common for interpreters to miss these subtle signals.

15a.   **When a lexical item is used for an utterance boundary, it is interpreted inaccurately.**

Utterance boundaries in ASL can be marked by using certain lexical items such as FINISH, PUSH-ASIDE or BUT, which signal the end of one utterance and the possibility of making another utterance. The signer says ME GO-TO STORE FINISH GO-TO LIBRARY. The interpreter says, "I've gone to the store and the library," instead of, "After I go to the store, I'm going to the library."

15b.   **When a pause is used for the utterance boundary, it is interpreted inaccurately.**

Boundaries can also be conveyed by pauses, which break up the discourse in much the same way as they do in spoken English. For example, ME-HELP-YOU WANT, CAN'T - the comma indicates a pause. In this instance, the speaker's unavailability is an additional thought, "I really want to help you, but I just can't." The interpreter misses this structure guide and says, "I can't help you," changing the emphasis.

15c.   **When an eye blink or head nod is used for the utterance boundary, it is interpreted inaccurately.**

Signers use eye blinks or head nods to identify ASL boundaries. Interpreters commonly miss the separation or relation of ideas the signer intends to convey, if they miss the "punctuation." It is important to note the head nod does not mean agreement. It is simply the end of the utterance.

15d. **When a shift in the physical stance of the body is made for the utterance boundary, it is interpreted inaccurately.**

Body shifts are used to introduce characterization but also to indicate time changes, which are often missed. For example, a slight body shift forward with the shoulder and chin slightly forward can indicate a time boundary, meaning a shift from the current tense to future tense. For example, the signer's message is ME READ NEWSPAPER NOW, READ BOOK. The interpreter misses the tense shift and says, "I am reading a book and the newspaper now," instead of, "I'm reading the newspaper now. Then, I will read the book."

15e. **When the signer's hands are used for the utterance boundary, it is interpreted inaccurately.**

A common misinterpretation, seen frequently in the research samples, occurs when signers lower their hands slightly to indicate a pause or a change of subject but the interpretation comes to a complete stop. At times, this is appropriate and the signer may really be indicating the end of a discourse. However, sometimes this movement is simply a short, necessary pause, and the signer intends to continue.

15f. **When a new topic is introduced, the interpretation is inaccurate.**

Interpreters frequently neglect to convey the meaning of utterance boundaries. The result is that information from the previous segment of the signer's discourse is misapplied to a subsequent section. So, overlooking utterance boundaries can lead to serious inaccuracies in the message interpreted. For example, a signer is discussing a marvelous trip to Hawaii and detailing what he liked about the various islands that he visited. When he went to the Big Island of Hawaii after staying a few days on Oahu, he was impressed with the quietness of the island. If the interpreter applied the "quietness" to "Oahu," because he or she missed the transition to the Big Island, the message was skewed. Oahu, where Waikiki is located, is anything but quiet!

16. **When the signer changes hand dominance (i.e., changes from right-handed signing to left-handed signing), the interpretation is accurate.**

Possible errors

16a. When the signer is left-handed, the interpretation is inaccurate: Left-handed fingerspelling is not captured.

16b. When the signer changes dominance back and forth from the left to the right hand during the discourse, the interpretation is inaccurate: An unexpected shift in hand dominance causes information to be missed.

16c. When the non-dominant hand is used for structuring space, the interpretation is inaccurate: Reference errors occur.

16d. When the non-dominant hand is used for emphasis, the interpretation is inaccurate: The signer fingerspells J-O-H-N with the dominant hand and points to the spelling with the non-dominant hand. The interpreter does not convey the special emphasis on "John."

Discussion

The non-dominant hand is commonly referred to as the passive hand. However, the term "passive hand" can be misleading. The passive hand is not inactive although it performs a different function from the dominant hand. It may be a very important function, such as clarifying or emphasizing.

16a.   When the signer is left-handed, the interpretation is inaccurate.

The vast majority of signers are right-handed, and therefore interpreters are used to interpreting for right-handed rather than left-handed signers. For some interpreters, it is more difficult to provide a quality interpretation for a left-handed signer. For example, if the signer is saying, "From east to west, we use French in Canada," he or she may sign WEST with the left hand followed by EAST with the right. The interpreter may miss the left-hand, WEST, and say, "In eastern Canada, we use French." In conveying the idea "east to west," a right-handed signer will most often start with the right hand, EAST, and then use the left hand, WEST, while a left-handed signer will do the opposite, start with the left hand, WEST, and then the right, EAST.

16b.   When the signer changes dominance back and forth from the left to the right hand during the discourse, the interpretation is inaccurate.

Some signers have a particular manner of signing that includes changing from left to right hand dominance and back again. For instance, he or she might sign HAT MY W-O-O-L using the right hand for HAT MY but fingerspelling W-O-O-L on the left. This unusual use of the non-dominant hand can be confusing. Interpreters would be expecting that the non-dominant hand would be used primarily for a particular reason, like conveying location or emphasis, not for unhighlighted information. More standard use of both hands by signers can also be difficult for interpreters to read. For example, when GIRL and BOY are discussed, GIRL is signed with the dominant hand and BOY is signed with the non-dominant hand. When the non-dominant hand is used, the information that it conveys may be omitted in the interpretation.

16c. **When the non-dominant hand is used for structuring space, the interpretation is inaccurate.**

One common use of the non-dominant hand is for structuring space. Often for example, the non-dominant hand may be used as a place-holder for a specific point such as a hotel where the signer stayed in Cape Town, South Africa. The dominant hand may then be used to show the direction and distance traveled during several short day excursions. The location in Cape Town will be central to describing each excursion, so the reference and relationship expressed by the non-dominant hand must be included in the interpretation.

16d. **When the non-dominant hand is used for emphasis, the interpretation is inaccurate.**

Often the non-dominant hand is used for emphasis. For example, when the dominant hand conveys a specific location, the non-dominant hand may also be used, perhaps subtly, by pointing with the index finger. This signing adds additional emphasis to a particular point in the discourse and should be conveyed by the interpreter.

Production:
English Lexicon

OVERVIEW

The last two sections grouped skills and common errors associated with comprehension of ASL, at the lexical and at the discourse levels. Now the analysis moves on to skills and errors associated with accuracy in the English target language message an interpreter uses, specifically vocabulary. The task here is to provide the bridge between two very differently structured languages. This often involves finding grammatically correct and meaningful expressions for elements of ASL that do not have direct equivalents in English. To achieve this, interpreters need a strong grasp of English word and structure choices. They are then well-equipped to say what the signer <u>means</u>, even if there is no way to say literally in English exactly what the signer signs in ASL.

17.	The interpretation is accurate when the signer uses ASL name signs.

Possible errors

17a. ASL name signs are interpreted with an explanation of what they look like: The interpreter says "P-handshape tapping on the left shoulder," a description of the movement, rather than saying, "Phyllis."

17b. When ASL name signs are used, an inaccurate name is used: The wrong individual is identified – "Peter" for "Paul."

17c. ASL name signs are replaced by generic terms: The interpreter says "this man" or "this woman" rather than the name of the individual.

17d. A name sign is interpreted as if it were an initialized sign or an adjective: The interpreter says "personnel" instead of "Patrice."

Discussion

Name signs are created for identifying and referring to specific individuals. They are often initialized, which means that the first initial of the person's name may be used, sometimes along with a reference to an outstanding characteristic of an individual like dimples or a birthmark.

A common discourse strategy in ASL is for signers to begin by identifying the person to whom they are referring and introducing a name sign that is specific to that individual. For example, if the person's name is Jane then the name sign only refers to that specific Jane, not all women with the name "Jane."

Of course, if the signer is in a community where people know each other by their name signs, then the signer will refer to these individuals by using the name sign alone. In such a situation, it is up to the interpreter to determine the name of the individual who is the topic of conversation and reflect this in the interpretation.

17a.   ASL name signs are interpreted with an explanation of what they look like.

With few exceptions, only a correct name or a pronoun referring to a precise individual should be included in the interpretation. No description of the individual's name sign (e.g., "C tapping on right side of forehead") should be included. Such a description would make no sense to a non-deaf audience. The use of name signs is a significant difference in usage between ASL and English. However, description of this ASL feature should <u>not</u> be part of an interpretation. An exception would be if "name signs" are a topic of conversation and the signer is providing examples of what name signs look like in ASL.

17b.   When ASL name signs are used, an inaccurate name is used.

Sometimes the name of an individual used in an interpretation is different from the one indicated by the name sign. For example, the name sign for "William Stokoe" is misinterpreted as "Dennis Cokely." The interpreter may know that the name sign refers to an internationally known individual, but may choose the wrong name. The name sign for Stokoe (with a "claw-handshape" at the temple) and Cokely (with a "D-handshape" moving across the forehead) are both articulated on the top half of the head. The interpreter may confuse the name signs and these two individuals.

ASL differs from English in that it does not use different name signs in different settings. Naming usage in English might change depending on the purpose, intent and context of the encounter. For example, in a formal setting such as an interview, it is more appropriate to refer to individuals as "Mr. McGill" and "Dr. Khaliq" rather than "Mike" and "Shameem." Even though, you, as the interpreter, may know these individuals on a first name basis, the interview setting is a formal interaction and the way in which participants are addressed may be important. English speakers use many different names for the same individual, for example, "Dr. Shifton," "Robert," "Bob," and "Bobby." "Dr. Shifton" might be used when introducing his keynote address. "Robert" might be used when referring to him in a meeting where he is known by others. "Bob" might be used in an office setting by his colleagues, and his best friends or his siblings might use "Bobby." All the names refer to the same individual but would be used in different settings and perhaps by different people. It may be considered disrespectful to use informal names in certain settings and with certain audiences. It would be inappropriate to introduce a guest speaker as "Bobby Shifton" rather than giving credentials by choosing to say, "Dr. Robert Shifton." (See also Register.)

Interpreters must know how to change a name sign into a name form appropriate for the setting. In this case, the interpreter would be adding information not provided by the signer's message, to conform to good usage in the target language.

17c.   ASL name signs are replaced by generic terms.

If name signs are used and the interpreter does not know to whom they refer, using generic terms is a possible strategy. At times, this may be the only solution available to interpreters, and it is better than not interpreting anything at all. However, it is still an error if an individual is not indicated clearly in the interpretation. The degree of specificity in ASL is not included in the English interpretation and equivalency is diminished.

17d.   A name sign is interpreted as if it were an initialized sign or an adjective:

Name signs can be misunderstood and misinterpreted. For example, a signer may talk about being in a store and seeing a friend. But the interpreter may miss the sign FRIEND and instead refer to a particular food on the shelf. Another example would be if a deaf person is talking about football and different teams like Edmonton Eskimos and Los Angeles Rams are discussed. The interpreter may miss the signs for these teams and instead interpret only the information about fouls committed, without conveying which team committed the fouls.

18.   The interpretation is accurate when the signer uses acronyms (AIDS pronounced as one word) and abbreviations (C-O-R-P voiced as "corporation").

Possible errors

18a. Letters or syllables are added or deleted in the interpretation: National Organization of Women (NOW) becomes "Northwest" if the "O" is missed.

18b. The acronym or abbreviation and its meaning is omitted from the interpretation.

18c. The acronym or abbreviation is expressed in a non-standard manner in the interpretation: R-I-D is said as one word, instead of three individual letters.

18d. The acronym or abbreviation is not said in full when the setting calls for this: B-C is not conveyed as "British Columbia" when interpreting for people from the eastern part of the United States who may not be familiar with western Canada and may need this information.

18e. The acronym or abbreviation is said in full when the signer first uses it but not linked to an acronym: The interpreter subsequently, uses the acronym without the referent, so the audience never gets the link between the acronym and what it stands for.

18f. The acronym or abbreviation is said in full the entire time when this is unnecessary: "The Association of Visual Language Interpreters of Canada" is used throughout a four-day annual conference instead of using the common acronym "AVLIC."

Discussion

Acronyms are closely related to abbreviations. They are "pronounceable abbreviations." They use initials from the words in the "source" name, and those letters are said as one word. Examples include the names of institutions and organizations, such as UNICEF (United Nations Children's Fund) or NATO (the North Atlantic Treaty Organization).

Abbreviations like OR for "operating room" may use the initial letter of each word in the phrase and identify each letter separately. Or, the letters may be combined into words. For example, a person may hear the acronym RID (Registry of Interpreters for the Deaf) pronounced as one word, "RID," in certain parts of the U.S., and may hear it referred to using three individual letters, "R" "I" "D," an abbreviation which is the correct form according to RID itself.

18a. **Letters or syllables are added or deleted in the interpretation.**

The meaning of all signed letters and syllables must be present in the interpretation. If any are added or deleted, it is considered an error. For example, if A-I-D-S is said as "AID" without an "s," then the meaning changes. Or, if an "s" is added to "NATO," it is also an error.

18b.   The acronym or abbreviation and its meaning is omitted from the interpretation.

The meaning of acronyms and/or abbreviations must be retained in the interpretation. At times the whole phrase may need to be expressed. For instance, M-R-C should be interpreted as "the Message Relay Center" for non-deaf audiences unfamiliar with this particular abbreviation.

18c.   The acronym or abbreviation is expressed in a non-standard manner in the interpretation.

It is important to know when acronyms and abbreviations are pronounced as words (e.g., NAFTA, UNIX) and when they are articulated as individual letters (e.g., UN, NTID). The Canadian Association of the Deaf (CAD) is pronounced as individual letters and not as one word. If it was pronounced as one word, it might be understood as "computer-aided design."

There are times when individual letter sounds and letters voiced as a word are combined. For example, California State University, Northridge (CSUN) has two common forms. In one, only the first letter "C" is named and followed by one word "SUN." In the other, four individual letters "C" "S" "U" "N" are articulated.

18d.   The acronym or abbreviation is not said in full when the setting calls for this.

Acronyms and abbreviations must have clear referents to make the message clear to the audience. For example, if interpreting in the local university community, it is a generally accepted principle to use an acronym or abbreviation for the institution rather than the full name. However, if interpreting about that same institution in another province or state, the interpretation needs to change to suit a "foreign" audience. An interpreter might say, the "University of Alberta has an excellent measurement and evaluation department. The faculty at U of A is renowned in this highly specialized field." Once the acronyms or abbreviations have been established, then "U of A" can be used throughout the remainder of the interpretation. If however, the referent is not clear, then "U of A" may need to be said in full once again, as the "University of Alberta." This is especially important if the acronym or abbreviation being used might be confused with a common local acronym. For example, "U of A" used in Arizona would be understood as the "University of Arizona," and not the "University of Alberta."

18e. **The acronym or abbreviation is said in full when the signer first uses it but not linked to an acronym.**

Another error that occurred fairly often in the research samples was failure to establish a relationship between a referent and an acronym or abbreviation. The referent must be used at the beginning of an utterance at least once, before the acronym can be used alone. For example, if the full name of the university is first used and then, several minutes later, only the abbreviation is used the cohesion between the full name and the abbreviation is lacking. The audience would be unable to determine what the abbreviation referred to.

18f. **The acronym or abbreviation is said in full the entire time when this is unnecessary.**

When an acronym or an abbreviation is not used, and instead the term is said in full every time, the interpretation can sound too formal. It would be unusual for "B.C." to be said in full to refer to centuries such as "500 B.C." It would sound strange to most audiences to hear "500 Before Christ...." Similarly, it would be unusual to say, "British Columbia" in full instead of "B.C." when referring to the western-most province of Canada, if the audience is Canadian or from the northwestern states.

19. Interpretation of ASL referencing is accurate. (See also Eye gaze.)

Possible errors

19a. Pronouns are used repeatedly instead of a combination of pronouns and the original referent(s): "He" is used several times to describe two men talking, causing difficulty for the audience in determining the referent for "he."

19b. Nouns are used repeatedly instead of pronouns: Proper names are overused: "Sheree said Wesley came in" and "Sheree said Wesley was in a hurry."

19c. Pronouns are used inaccurately when the signer does not specify a gender in ASL: The nurse is referred to as "her" when in fact the nurse is a man.

19d. First person and third person are used inconsistently: The signer says in first person ME VISIT F-R-E-D TOMORROW. The interpreter switches to third person and says, "He says he'll visit Fred tomorrow."

19e. Interpretation is unclear or inaccurate about a referent: When the interpreter says, "The cat is by the mat. Did you see it?" The "it" could be the cat or the mat.

Discussion

19a.   **Pronouns are used repeatedly instead of a combination of pronouns and the original referent(s).**

Every time pronouns are used, their referents must be clear. It is considered an error, for instance, when the signer refers to two characters of the same gender and the interpretation uses "he" for both people. For example, the interpreter says, "First he said he wanted it, then <u>he</u> said he'd get it" sounds as if there is just one man involved. The signer, for instance, may have meant "John wanted it, and Mike said he would get it for him." Once the referent and the pronoun that refers to it are established, it is sometimes necessary to repeat the noun, rather than constantly using the pronoun. When a pronoun is used excessively, it becomes repetitive and the signer's message can lose its clarity and impact.

19b.   Nouns are used repeatedly instead of pronouns.

The opposite of the above error can also occur. If nouns are used repeatedly, instead of substituting pronouns occasionally, an awkward interpretation is produced in English. For example, in English you would not hear:
"Ramona skis in Banff, but Ramona doesn't like skiing in Aspen because Ramona finds the States too expensive."
Instead the pronoun "she" would be used:
"Ramona skis in Banff, but she doesn't like skiing in Aspen because she finds the States too expensive."

19c.   Pronouns are used inaccurately when the signer does not specify a gender in ASL.

It is important for interpreters to note items like occupations where gender assumptions occur. Are doctors and lawyers referred to in the interpretation as men, and nurses and teachers referred to as women? Interpreters have to be aware of their own potential for bias in choosing pronouns for their target language message. Although there is still a tendency in some fields to have a higher percentage of men or of women, it is dangerous for interpreters to make these assumptions. Neutral terms should be used to express meaning whenever possible. For example instead of terms such as "waiter," "stewardess," and "chairman," terms such as "server," "flight attendant," and "chairperson" can be chosen. This avoids the risk of using sexist language.

At times one must choose a gender in English. If a person is spoken about at length in English without specifying the gender, it sounds suspicious. English speakers can only use terms such as "this person" or "my roommate" for a limited period of time before it begins to sound evasive. For example, in a counseling session a deaf client is talking about his roommate and constantly refers to his roommate by using his index finger to point. If the interpreter continues to say, "roommate" and avoids specifying a gender for the person, the counselor may assume the deaf client is trying to avoid identifying whether he lives with a man or a woman. In fact, it does not matter to the deaf client and this apparent "vagueness" is simply a function of the fact that in ASL gender is not necessarily specified. Extensive awkward circumlocution or incorrect pronoun use, such as using "they" to refer to a single person, to avoid gender clarity is worse than attributing gender.

It may be impossible to interrupt the signer to find out the gender of the individual being talked about. In such cases, the interpreter may make an informed guess and be ready to correct it later. This kind of choice is imposed by different usage in each language. When possible interpreters should talk with the signer in advance to find out information that may be relevant to the interpretation, such as the gender of cousins and doctors mentioned. This is also an opportunity for interpreters and deaf people to work together to improve an interpretation. Sometimes it is important to assist the deaf person to understand the differences between ASL and English and suggest ways the signer can participate helpfully in the interpretation process.

19d.   First person and third person are used inconsistently.

Pronouns must be used correctly to identify those speaking (using first person) and those spoken about (using third person). For example, a child is talking about the way her mother treats her, and uses characterization. But the interpreter says, "I am treated like a child by my mother. She always talks down to her." The interpreter's switch to "her" sounds as if a different daughter, another person, is being spoken about. Another example occurs when the signer uses first person possessive, "my" wife, when he introduces his spouse. The interpreter also uses first person, "my wife," instead of switching to the third person possessive "his wife." It sounds as if the interpreter is married to the signer's wife.

19e.   Interpretation is unclear or inaccurate about a referent.

Pronouns such as "they" and "it" must refer clearly to the nouns they replace. For example, in the sentence, "Miguel and Tanya told Norbert and Jack they were not invited." It is not clear to whom "<u>they</u>" refers; is it Miguel and Tanya or Norbert and Jack?

Sometimes a referent is understood in ASL from the context, but must be clearly added to the English interpretation. For example, the signer has been talking about his favorite team, the Seattle Seahawks and how they're doing in the series. To ASL signers it's clear that the person is talking about <u>his</u> team by the way the SCORE information is signed. He might sign TEAM WON SIX THREE where the signing of SIX is close to the body and THREE is away from the body. The interpreter must add the referent "<u>our</u> team won six to three," to provide message equivalency for an English-speaking audience.

If the pronoun used can not clearly be related to its referent, then the <u>noun should be repeated</u>. For example, in the sentence, "To prevent dogs from chewing on shoes, soak them in a special solution provided by the vet," are the dogs or the shoes to be soaked? When the pronoun "them" is replaced with "the shoes," the sentence becomes clear: "To prevent dogs from chewing on shoes, soak the shoes in a special solution provided by the vet."

Most of the time, when a signer is referring to a physical item visible to the audience, ASL reference pronouns such as THIS and THAT are used. Often, however, due to the sequential nature of ASL-English interpretation, the signer is no longer indicating THIS or THAT when it is interpreted. When the timing is off, the audience becomes confused. One solution is for the interpretation to include the noun to which the signer referred such as "the door behind you" or the "bulletin board up front," instead of "this" or "that."

20. A diverse range of vocabulary and accurate selection of English lexical items is used.

Possible errors

20a. Lexical choices are limited: There is no depth to the vocabulary used; it is simplistic when the signer is being eloquent.

20b. Particular lexical choices are overused: The interpreter repeatedly uses "so" or "and then."

20c. The target message contains redundancy: Different words that say the same thing are used in combinations such as "uniquely special."

20d. English idioms are used inaccurately: "You're a sight for sore eyes," is used in a negative sense when its meaning is positive.

20e. ASL lexical intrusions are present: "For, for" is said instead of "reason." "King Burger" is said instead of "Burger King."

20f. Non-standard lexical choices are made: The signer talks about where his seat was for the basketball game and the interpreter says, "theater-style seating" instead of the more appropriate choice, "bleachers."

Discussion

Interpreters must have an extensive English lexical and grammatical base to render effective interpretations. They must also have any technical vocabulary required for the particular settings in which they work (e.g., computing science, linguistics or physics). It is also helpful to know slang for some situations. However, it is a mistake to pick rare or fancy words if they are not needed to convey a signer's precise meaning. In general, using vocabulary that is unusual will cause the audience to focus on the interpretation and not on the signer's message.

20a.   Lexical choices are limited.

The words the interpreter chooses must reflect the signer's intent. The research samples showed that one of the most frequent errors is a limited use of English vocabulary when the signer is being eloquent. When simple language, using one- or two-syllable words, is chosen, the subtleties and precision in the source language message are lacking. For instance, the signer says, "I am intrigued," and the interpreter says, "I wanted to know."

20b.   Particular lexical choices are overused.

Repetition usually weakens sentences and therefore weakens the overall message. Interpreters often tend to repeat words like "and," "very," "truly," "well" and "quite." An example would be "It was <u>quite</u> pretty outside and I <u>quite</u> enjoyed it."

Repetition can simply be a bad speaking habit. An interpreter may overuse a stock phrase like "and next we will discuss..." It is better to introduce new topics in a variety of ways – "next on the agenda" or "I would like to direct your attention to. . ." It may be acceptable to use the repetition if the signer is doing so for emphasis or rhythm. However, that would be an exception to the general rule.

20c.   The target message contains redundancy.

Interpreters may repeat words exactly (i.e., repetition), or they may change the words, but repeat an idea (i.e. redundancy). For example in the phrase "unemployed workers who are not working..." the audience gets one piece of information twice because "unemployed workers" by definition are "not working." Redundant phrases are also a problem but might be less obvious. Examples include, "new updated information," "consensus of shared opinion," and "large in size." In all of these examples, the first word is sufficient for conveying the information. The remaining words are redundant and should not be tacked on.

Redundancy can be used intentionally in English as in ASL for emphasis or rhythm. It is important to know how it is used in each language. If the signer is being redundant on purpose, the interpretation should be redundant as well.

20d.   English idioms are used inaccurately.

Use of idioms allows interpreters to make full use of the expressive possibilities of English. For example, idioms such as "come rain or come shine" can be used very effectively in English for the sign IT-DOESN'T-MATTER. Idioms must be used accurately and it is important not to confuse two or more idiomatic expressions. For example, it is inaccurate to say, "that's a <u>cow</u> of a different color," instead of, "that's a <u>horse</u> of a different color."

20e.   ASL lexical intrusions are present.

ASL must be interpreted into an acceptable English semantic form. It is not acceptable to interpret "Holland language" for "Dutch" or "the round heavy thing" for a "medicine ball." ASL lexical intrusions are common hazards in interpretations as the interpreter follows the signing. Sometimes the intrusions are fairly minor but noticeable. An example would be repeating in English the signed sequence of KING BURGER for the fast-food restaurant, instead of correctly transposing it to "Burger King." The sequence in which signs are produced in ASL may differ from sequences used in English. If the interpreter doesn't make these slight appropriate adjustments, the variations may reflect negatively on the signer and reduce the effectiveness of the presentation, although they do not lose the audience completely. For example, an interpreter might convey PEPPER SALT as "pepper and salt," instead of the more common "salt and pepper."

Sometimes retaining ASL structure can produce incomprehensible target language messages. For example, interpreting TRAIN-GONE as "the train is gone" instead of "You're too late" would baffle an English speaking audience.

20f.   Non-standard lexical choices are made.

Sometimes there is no easy match between an ASL sign with its visual information component and an English word. Interpreters must develop skill in anticipating and responding to these situations. A wide English vocabulary will help an interpreter to achieve equivalency. For example, if the signer is judging the freshness of a fish, he or she might indicate the condition of the eyes of the fish. The interpreter would need to be able to find an appropriate word for the visual image, like the word "concave" which may not easily spring to mind.

As in any language, ASL signs are occasionally less precise or technical than "equivalent" English words. For example, a signer will indicate that an animal has in injury by signing GOAT F-O-O-T, PAIN. The interpreter must choose "goat's hoof" instead of "goat's foot" or "goat's paw."

21. The English interpretation is grammatically accurate.

Possible errors

21a. Subject and verb agreement is inaccurate: The interpreter says, "Beads and thread <u>is</u> used to make necklaces," instead of "are."

21b. Pronouns do not agree in person and/or number with their referent: The interpreter says, "If a <u>person</u> studies hard, <u>they</u> can pass the test" using the plural third person "they" instead of the singular form "he" or "she."

21c. Non-standard English is used: The interpreter says, "Playing <u>real well</u> is the goal of hockey practice" when "real well" should be replaced with the correct adverb use, "really well."

21d. Incomplete sentences are used: "Deaf people like to go to deaf schools and are not interested in going to hearing." The sentence should end with the word "schools."

21e. Tense is changed haphazardly: "I was going along and then I see John," is used instead of, "I was going along and then I <u>saw</u> John."

Discussion

A full discussion of English grammar is beyond the scope of this book. However, it is important for interpreters to gradually strengthen their English grammar knowledge and skills to improve the quality of their interpretation work. In this section, a few commonly encountered errors are noted.

21a.   Subject and verb agreement is inaccurate.

Singular subjects require singular verbs. Plural subjects require plural verbs. When sentences contain clauses or phrases between subject and verb, it is a common error to make the verb agree with the closest noun or pronoun, instead of the subject. For example, "a box of <u>nails</u>, if you drop <u>them</u>, <u>are</u> going to spill everywhere," should be "a <u>box</u> of nails, if you drop <u>it</u>, <u>is</u> going to spill everywhere." A number of words in English like "none" and "a group" take singular verbs although they seem to refer to several objects. It is correct to say, "A group of people is going," although "several <u>people are</u> going" is right, too.

Sometimes the meaning of a sentence is only made clear by the subject/verb plural agreement. Here is an example:
o "People pick up information from books that <u>keep</u> them informed." If "keep" is plural, it refers to the plural noun "books" meaning "<u>books keep</u> them informed."
o "People pick up information from books that keeps them informed." If "keeps" is singular, it refers to the singular noun "information," meaning "<u>information keeps</u> them informed."

21b.   Pronouns do not agree in person and/or number with their referent.

Interpreters must be careful not to shift for no reason between first-, second-, and third-person pronouns and between singular and plural forms of these pronouns. In the ungrammatical example "If a <u>student</u> studies hard, <u>they</u> can achieve great things," the singular noun, "student," can not be referred to with the plural third-person pronoun, "they," in the second half of the sentence.

21c.   Non-standard English is used.

The standard for spoken English varies from region to region. It is important to know what is acceptable and what is common in the region(s) where one works. Non-standard adverb use like saying, "Friends take each other <u>serious</u>," or, "you did real well," is common, but the grammatically correct usage would be to say, "seriously" and "really." Non-standard verb usage like, "I'll borrow you ten dollars," is often not acceptable. "I'll lend you ten dollars," should be used if interpreting for a native English speaking audience. When non-standard verbs or English structure are used in the interpretation it reflects poorly on the signer.

21d.   Incomplete sentences are used.

Incomplete sentences occurred most often in the research samples at the beginning of an interpretation, or when new topics were introduced. Interpreters, caught up in the signing, may think they have voiced complete sentences, when in fact, they have left ideas unfinished. For example, the interpreter says, "The book has to be researched. Which is a big job." Here, a clause is made to stand in for a complete sentence. A better interpretation would be, "The book has to be researched. <u>It</u> is a big job." In general, sentences in an

103

interpretation should be complete unless for some reason an incomplete sentence is the intent of the signer. Each sentence should have at least a subject and a verb. If one of these is not present, it is an error. Of course, there are exceptions. For example, one word answers to questions may be acceptable. But in general, all sentences must include a subject and a verb as a minimal requirement.

Although one-word answers can be used appropriately in English, it is often better to interpret a one-word statement or question as a complete sentence. For example, if LATER is signed in answer to a question about whether or not the people at the meeting want to take a break, it would be better to provide a complete sentence such as "I'd like to take a break later."

21e.   Tense is changed haphazardly.

Unless otherwise stated, one can assume that a topic is expressed in the present tense in ASL, if no other indication is given. Usually when past or future tense is intended, a time indicator will be used. For example, to denote past tense, signs like YESTERDAY, LAST-YEAR and LONG-TIME-AGO may be used. Signs to represent future tense include TOMORROW, NEXT-WEEK AND WILL. Once time/tense has been established, everything following retains that tense, until a change is made.

In interpretations of ASL signing, English verb tense should not switch from past to present to future unless this is specifically indicated by the signer. A common error found in the research samples was that interpreters accurately conveyed tense at the beginning of the text, but then, later, changed tense in the interpretation, when it did not change in the ASL source message. For example, the deaf person was talking about the errands she did yesterday. The interpretation accurately started off in the past tense and then by the third and fourth errand changed to the future tense. (See also Temporal aspect.)

Production:
English Discourse

OVERVIEW

English, like other languages, is dynamic and interactive. Usage changes from culture to culture, region to region and from context to context. Skilled speakers can easily handle a vast range of speech situations by drawing on the richness and flexibility of the language. They can produce formal discourse, or chat with friends. They can blend in colorful "slang" or describe a complex technical process. This level of language use requires "knowledge-rich" skills. These include sensitivity to different elements of the context of an interpretation, like the cultural or educational backgrounds of the participants. Knowledge-rich speakers can choose from a range of expressive options in English in any given situation.

For interpreters, these knowledge-rich skills must rest on a firm foundation in the knowledge-lean skills discussed so far in the text – understanding ASL lexicon and ASL discourse, and mastering English lexicon and grammar. If interpreters make frequent or serious errors in these knowledge-lean skill areas, errors will probably also crop up at the English discourse level. This section focuses on the skill areas interpreters need to produce high-caliber English discourse. The goal is to provide target messages that are equivalent to the source message and that are clear, accurate and interesting to the English-speaking audience.

22. **The English interpretation avoids ASL intrusions. (See also Vocabulary range.)**

Possible errors

22a. ASL syntactic intrusions are present in the interpretation: ASL rhetorical structure is retained. The interpreter says, "You should show up on time, why?" instead of "The reason you should show up on time is ...."

22b. ASL signs are glossed inappropriately in the interpretation: The signer says #CAR WE-THREE ALL-GET-IN DRIVE+++ and the interpreter settles for "We all got into the car and <u>drove, drove, drove</u>."

22c. Descriptions of signs are provided: The interpreter actually says, "f-hand on the forehead." (See also Name signs.)

Discussion

22a. ASL syntactic intrusions are present in the interpretation.

ASL syntactic intrusions were documented frequently in the research samples. One common example was the production of awkward English sentence structures because bracketing strategy in ASL sentence construction was retained in the interpretation. For example in ASL one might sign ME THINK, GO MALAYSIA, ME THINK. The interpretation is awkward if the bracketing is retained, "I think I will go to Malaysia, I think." Instead, possible interpretations, depending on the context, would be "I am considering going to Malaysia, but I am not sure yet," or "I am thinking about going to Malaysia." The point is to avoid retaining ASL forms when these structures are either not used in English or not used in the same way in English. It is important to note that the content may be understandable, but the communication process will be affected. If these errors occur regularly, the signer will sound inarticulate and the awkward interpretation structures will significantly influence the audience's perception of him or her. Another example would be retaining ASL structure, "he smiled and I smiled" rather than switching to English syntax to say, "we smiled at each other."

Rhetorical questions are used in ASL for emphasis, whereas in English they may be used to solicit audience involvement and attention. In most cases rhetorical question structure in ASL should be communicated as a statement in English. For example RIVER OVERFLOW, WHY? RAIN RAIN RAIN MOUNTAINS might be interpreted in English as, "Due to heavy rainfall in the mountains, the river is overflowing," or "The river is overflowing because of heavy rainfall in the mountains." However, rhetorical questions sometimes are retained. If for instance, the signer is communicating instructions to a new employee, the English interpretation, "What should you do if you cannot show up to work? Call Juan," would be appropriate.

Another kind of ASL syntactic intrusions occurs when verbs are left hanging at the end of English sentences. To avoid this, the ASL structure needs to be converted into a more common English usage. For example, YOU ME WILL MOVIE GO, is stated in English as "You and I will go to the movie." It would be wrong to keep ASL syntactic structure and say, "You and I will movie go." It is also a grammar error if the ASL "you/me" structure intrudes into the English sentence: "You and me will go to the movie." Tag questions, a common structure in ASL, should be used sparingly in English. They weaken the statement to which they are attached. For example, "I am a good driver, don't you think?" or "Two-year interpreting programs are too short, aren't they?"

22b.   ASL signs are glossed inappropriately in the interpretation.

Another common error noted in the research samples was "verbatim" translation, or glossing of ASL signs into English. For example, if an interpreter follows ASL usage by repeating signs, the interpretation will contain the very awkward English phrasing like "again, again, again," instead of correct construction using an <u>adverb</u> like "repeatedly" or "frequently." In this example, the audience can still comprehend the intended message, but that is not always the case. In ASL usage, FOR FOR means "because," "why?" or "what is that?" That meaning is lost, however, if the ASL intrusion is retained in English and the interpreter says, "For, for?" instead of "Why?" Verbatim translations also cause errors in tone. For example, the signer says ME-INFORM-YOU and the interpretation uses this stern, almost angry-sounding phrase instead of softening it appropriately for politeness to, "just to let you know."

Problems also emerge with compound signs, like THINK⌒SELF. If the interpreter uses these exact words "think self," a non-signing audience probably won't get the message, "It is up to you," or, "It is your decision." *109*

Repetition of one or more signs is fairly common at the end of ASL questions. However such repetition is unusual in English. It would, for instance, be uncommon to hear "Who is he? Who is he?" twice (unless the signer had some cause to be frantic). Unfortunately, some interpreters retain the ASL form when they see repetition and tend to voice the structure of the ASL utterance rather than interpreting its meaning into a form appropriate for English listeners.

22c.   Descriptions of signs are provided.

Another ASL intrusion error is including the description of signs in an interpretation from ASL to English. The average English audience does not know what "f-handshapes" or "x-handshapes" are. This was noted before in connection with name-sign equivalency. Signers may fingerspell a name and then add the phrase "F-handshape on forehead." The fact that a name sign was used is not relevant to an English audience. The audience needs to know <u>who</u> is referred to but not <u>how</u> the person was indicated in ASL.

A variant of this intrusion problem, involves attempting to voice ASL non-manual markers. For example, the signer conveys BOOK ME READ BIG (BIG is accompanied with the non-manual CHA meaning "very long") and the interpreter says, "That book I'm reading is cha."

23. Appropriate English discourse strategies are used to handle linguistic/cultural differences between ASL and English.

Possible errors

23a. The high level of visual detail in ASL is inappropriately retained in the interpretation: The interpreter says, "I was sitting at one end of the round table," instead of "I was sitting at the table." "Round" and is not required in the English interpretation

23b. Use of direct and/or indirect dialogue is inconsistent with the tone of the interaction being interpreted: The signer conveys, "He told me, 'Don't go there,'" and the interpreter fails to convert this to, "He told me not to go there," which would be more appropriate in English.

23c. In interpreting direct discourse, third person is used instead of first person: The interpreter says, "My mom called her son," when the signer is the son, instead of, "My mom called me." (See also Referencing.)

23d. ASL cultural information is interpreted inaccurately: The signer says SHE TALK NICE, BUT MEAN BEHIND NEGATIVE and the interpreter retains this "story line" instead of finding a cultural equivalent like, "left-handed compliment."

Discussion

Because English is so different in structure and history from ASL, interpreters need to develop real sensitivity to differences between the two languages and plan strategies for rendering discourse that meets the needs of both signer and audience.

23a.   The high level of detail in ASL is inappropriately retained in the interpretation.

The amount of detail provided in ASL is often greater than is needed in English. When too much information is interpreted into English, it can sound silly or inappropriate to English-speaking listeners. Such interpretation actually misrepresents the intent of the signer. For example, a Deaf man is talking about classmates of his who have passed away since he graduated 35 years ago from a residential school. In ASL he signs, UP-TILL-NOW HALF MY CLASS DEAD, CANCER, BRAIN T-U-M-O-R, STROKE, HEART-ATTACK. An acceptable interpretation is "Half of my classmates have died of various problems such as cancer and brain tumors," rather than interpreting all the specific causes of death. This translation choice correctly assumes that the specifics are not the point of the discussion. In English one or two examples are often sufficient. It is often difficult for interpreters to know how and when to shift from very specific to less specific accounts that suit an English audience.

23b.   **Use of direct and/or indirect dialogue is inconsistent with the tone of the interaction being interpreted.**

Another clear area of difference between English and ASL arises from their relative use of direct address (i.e., direct quotation or role-playing). Direct address is more common in ASL than in English. ASL signers use direct address frequently. In English it is acceptable but less common to use direct address (e.g. "She said, 'Stop!'"). It would be used occasionally in settings like story telling or comedy, but not in formal lectures. In formal lectures indirect address is used more frequently, "She told me to stop."

23c.   **In interpreting direct discourse, third person is used instead of first person.**

The use of first and third person in ASL and English is different. ASL uses first person much more often — for instance, when the signer is using characterization and role shifts to convey ideas for which English speakers would use indirect discourse. The signer may sign YESTERDAY, ME SEE B-R-E-N-T. ME is signed in first person. And then the signer may actually take on the role of Brent (first person) being shocked to run across his friend. In both instances, the signer is using first person when taking on the characters. The English interpretation needs to use both first and third person to relay this information saying something like "I (first person) saw Brent yesterday and he (third person) was shocked to see me (first person)."

23d.   **ASL cultural information is interpreted inaccurately.**

There are significant cultural differences in terms of need for context between ASL and English. For example, among English speakers, large amounts of information are "understood" or conveyed by syntax choices, word choices and other means. In ASL, context is often made explicit using several examples, characterization and so on. Interpreters must be sensitive to these structure and usage differences so they can provide a target language message appropriate for an English speaking audience.

Signers often provide rich context for their information. If interpreted word for word, the message does not sound the same in English and may seem condescending to the English speaking audience that is not expecting to be told "everything." The result is that the intent of the message and thus the equivalency of meaning are altered. English speakers will usually add extra context and details when speaking to children or to people trying to function in an unfamiliar environment.

Interpreters must also understand that non-deaf audiences do not necessarily have wide knowledge of deaf culture. Content that is clear and specific for a signer may need to be explained or elaborated for an audience. For example, culturally laden phrases for deaf people like "residential school," meaning a special facility for deaf students, may have an unclear meaning for the audience. English speakers may be making associations with expensive private schools or with the oppressive schooling system devised for Native-American children. Jokes are another kind of communication which requires careful, culturally-sensitive interpretation. For example, a signer may simply indicate B-U-T J-O-K-E. The interpreter needs to know that the "but" joke refers to a story about a deaf person trying to communicate with a non-deaf person about a train crossing. The non-deaf audience members will need to have that context provided or they may hear "butt" jokes.

If a person is being addressed in ASL and is present in the setting, the signer usually points with the index finger; in other words, the signer uses a pronoun. In contrast, English speakers tend to avoid "pointing," even "metaphorical" pointing achieved by using pronouns, if the person in question is present. English speakers tend to use people's names to refer to them when they are present. Interpreters must produce discourse that respects these cultural sensitivities.

113

The age and background of the signer may also provide an interpretation challenge, because cultural interpretation changes over time. For example, an elderly woman might sign FRIEND++ to refer to people at work when today it would be more appropriate to substitute "colleagues" in the interpretation.

24. **The register used in the interpretation matches the audience, the context and the signer's intent. (See also English discourse strategies.)**

Possible errors

24a. The message conveyed is inaccurately formal:
The interpreter tries to be "extra" correct and draws attention to him or herself.

24b. The message conveyed is inaccurately informal:
The interpreter uses language appropriate for friends in a formal lecture situation.

24c. The message conveyed is inconsistent in register:
The interpreter switches between "high brow" and "down home" styles without reason.

24d. The interpretation does not provide the necessary adjustments to register to make a good connection between the signer and the audience: The interpreter knows the English-speaking audience is unfamiliar with the "frankness" of ASL communication. He or she doesn't manage to adjust the target message to the "politeness norms" of English speakers.

24e. The lexicon chosen does not suit the setting: Jargon is used that is unfamiliar to the audience.

Discussion

"Register" is a term used by linguists to name all those things people can accomplish in signing or speaking, besides giving factual information. Signers and speakers use language, for instance, to exchange clues about each other's social, economic or age status. This information is not given overtly, but "shows" in the word choice, syntax, speech rhythms, and so on that are part of every communication.

Variations in register define the degree of formality or informality of an interaction. A signer will therefore choose a register in ASL that corresponds to the effect he or she wants to have on an audience. He or she would sign differently to a friend than to a visiting celebrity. Elements of register include politeness, or attention to etiquette, word choice, assertiveness, degree of complexity in phrasing, etc. These choices need to be appropriate for a particular setting. The register of signing would be different, for instance, in a law court than in a play school. "Register" is one of the ways members of a society determine and express the status of communicators, and reinforce or challenge hierarchies in social relations. Paralinguistic features such as intonation, pausing, and rate of signing/speaking vary with the register chosen. (See Production: Public Speaking.)

Variations in Register

"Frozen" register is found in ritualized speech forms like prayers, and anthems. These discourses express general membership in a large collective like a nationality or religious group. Strictly speaking it is not possible to interpret "frozen" texts. Once an interpreter's choices are included, the source text is no longer fixed. Because ASL is a relatively "new" language, there are very few examples of frozen text. Interpreters moving from English to ASL would have far more encounters with sections of frozen text in the source language. For instance, there is no set ASL version of the Lord's Prayer or the national anthem. One can "interpret" the meaning, but not the exact wording which is the frozen aspect of the text. One possible example of ASL frozen discourse is the "Bison" song of Gallaudet University. If this song were part of a signer's message, the interpreter might just say, "The signer is referring to the Gallaudet song." It would be better not to attempt an interpretation of the "frozen" ASL signs into their "perceived" English equivalents.

"Formal" register would be chosen if a speaker or signer is showing or claiming respect, or confirming existing social hierarchy. In these situations, the <u>way</u> information is presented is more strongly influenced by conventions, than by the speaker's personality. Examples might be lectures, interactions with employers or people of an older generation. Formal register is characterized by:

o fewer false starts;
o more complete utterances as sentences are carefully constructed;
o extended pauses;
o clear articulation and pronunciation;
o more complex syntax;
o longer sentences using compound structures and subordinate clauses; and,
o speaking deliberately.

"Informal" register would be chosen for talking with friends or peers. It is characterized by:

o less complex syntax;
o a faster speaking rate with more contractions, (e.g., "can't" and "hasn't");
o more assimilations (e.g., sounds influenced by proximity to other sounds like "don't you" becoming "don't ya"); and,
o shorter pauses.

Distinctions between formal and informal registers can be expressed through word choice, as in these examples:

Formal: "Following instruction on the computer, Mr. Thomas William's performance improved."
Informal: "After some computer lessons Tom did way better."

Formal: "Tom's focus is to acquire wealth rapidly."
Informal: "Tom's a sucker for 'get rich quick' schemes."

A longer example of formal register is:
"Allow me to explain why the international horse jumping competition that normally takes place annually at Spruce Meadows is not going to take place this year."

An informal way to say the same thing is:

"You know the horse jumping competition? The international one that happens every year? This year it it's not happening, and I'll tell you why."

24a.   The message conveyed is inaccurately formal.

Some interpreters have a natural formality when they speak. It may be difficult for interpreters whose natural speech patterns are formal to reach an informal register. If, for example, the signer is conducting an informal presentation, it would be inappropriate for the interpreter to use formal register. If the signer says NO ME NOT-WANT and the interpreter says, "No, I would prefer to not participate in this matter," it would be an error in register. "I don't want to," would be a better choice of words.

Other inaccuracies in the use of formal register arise for interpreters who are naturally informal speakers. They may have trouble making formal register sound right. For example, a deaf person is interviewing for a promotion. The signer says, "This job is part of my long-term career plan and I have upgraded all of my technical skills to prepare for it." Here, the signer has successfully used formal register to present herself to the hiring committee. It would be an error to shift the signer's directness and confidence into an arrogant tone, when trying to achieve formality. If, the interpreter says, "I've always known that such a position would reflect my capabilities appropriately. I've done everything necessary to meet your needs," an inaccurate picture of the signer's attitude is given. In this case, the interpreter is trying to sound formal, but is adding an element of pretension and pompousness instead. Achieving formal register is not just a question of stringing together 50-cent words. In fact, this approach can convey the opposite "register message" – namely, that the interpreter or the signer is really out of his or her depth.

A speaker using formal register may achieve elegance with very simple words. For example, the signer may be saying, "for indeed, truth really is beauty, and beauty truth." The signer expects that the audience will recognize this idea, and it is therefore "safe" to make a very short but elegant allusion to it. The formal register chosen by the signer would not in this case be conveyed with fancy words. "Aesthetics are indispensable to the signification of meaning and vice versa," does not

117

capture the signer's formality or expertise. It is useful to remember that even formal register should sound "natural."

24b.   The message conveyed is inaccurately informal.

Problems with using informal register often occur when the interpreter is too nervous to achieve an informal relaxed tone. If for example, the signer is chatting with members of her sports team, her signs may be produced in a more relaxed manner, often near the waist. Signs may be formed less distinctly and at a faster pace. The interpreter should respond by using a conversational tone in the English message. As in ASL, informal English is faster-paced than formal speech and more likely to include contractions, looser articulation and very current vocabulary. It would be inappropriate to try to produce a more crafted or polished discourse.

Interpreters must always be sensitive to context. It's wrong to fall back on an informal style in structured environments like a lecture hall, a presentation, or a social ritual like a marriage ceremony. In these environments some degree of formality is usually required.

24c.   The message conveyed is inconsistent in register.

During any particular discourse, the signer may switch between formal and less formal register. Even on formal occasions, a range of register will probably be used. It is an error to change registers when the signer does not do so or maintain the same register when the signer changes. For example, a signer may begin in a formal manner by introducing the topic and the plan for a one-hour presentation. The <u>choice</u> of formal register here subtly conveys that the signer doesn't wish to be interrupted with questions or comments. If, in contrast, the interpretation starts in an informal style, the audience may perceive that they are invited to participate. If the interpreter then switches to formal register the audience will be confused.

It is important that interpreters learn to change registers to follow the signer's message and intent. They may have to develop their own speaking abilities to accomplish this. "Fluidity" in changing register requires broad general knowledge and significant exposure to different settings and different people.

24d.   The interpretation does not provide the necessary adjustments to register to make a good connection between the signer and the audience.

Interpreters must be "culturally competent" in both ASL and English to assist an audience in understanding the intent of a signer. The interpreter is a bridge between the signer's discourse and the audience's capacity to follow that signer's ideas. For example, a signer may be discussing a student's philosophy paper. He may fingerspell a Latin word like *non-sequitur* in his comments. If the interpreter knows that the audience is mostly high school students with a limited background in philosophy, he or she might choose not to voice "non-sequitur." It would be better to "adjust" the signer's register slightly and substitute a phrase like, "the paper didn't flow well." In this case it is more important to take account of the comprehension level of the audience than to be "faithful" to the signer's fingerspelling.

NOTE: There is always an element of choice in these situations, and there are different philosophies about interpreting fingerspelled words. Some people in the field of interpretation, both educators and deaf consumers, feel strongly that when a signer chooses to fingerspell English, or, in this case, Latin words, these words must be retained in the interpretation.

Interpreters must have a thorough knowledge of how register is used in ASL. Here are some examples:

119

o   In ASL it is not disrespectful to include personal comments about someone's looks in signed discourse. It is simply a way to identify an idea in a visual language. However, any direct interpretation of these comments would be rude. The interpreter here has to decide how to balance between the information content the signer is generating and formal standards of politeness in English.

o In ASL quick "asides" are often used to give background information. This structure can pose problems for interpreters because English speakers often use the same structure to be "snarky." For example, the signer uses NOT-KNOW-ANYTHING with an F-handshape at the forehead. The interpreter must understand that the signer is not being insulting. It would be wrong to say, "Juan knows <u>zip</u> about football," when the signer means, "Juan is not familiar with football."

o When a Deaf teenager is applying to university and being interviewed by a group of non-deaf academics, the interpreter might choose to avoid using slang in the target language. For example, the signer uses a derogatory slang sign ("I" on the nose) when commenting that he wasn't ready for university last year. It would be wrong for the interpreter to use a similar "put down" in English like "real baby" instead of substituting a more formal word like "immature." In this case it is most important for the interpreter to allow the signer to make an appropriate connection with the admissions committee.

o There are several ways speakers' register can be subtly lowered by interpreters. For instance, interpreters may produce vague sentences when they don't fully understand the signer. The target message may be full of fillers like "I think" or "kind of" which make the signer sound less competent or less professional. Use of direct address also lowers register in English but not in ASL, where it is regularly used.

24e.   **The lexicon chosen does not suit the setting.**

The specific word choices (i.e., vocabulary) used in an interpretation must be consistent with the register of the signer's message <u>and</u> the context. For example if the signer uses professional jargon, the interpreter must be confident that the audience is familiar with the terminology. For instance, an audience outside the school system may not understand phrases like "Eighty per-cent of you have a <u>four-point</u> (meaning "straight A") record."

Another error would be to use legalistic words or phrases like "it is incumbent on me to ..." when interpreting for a trucker's union meeting.

25. **English cohesion markers, like pauses and transitions within and between sentences, tie the message together.**

Possible errors

25a. Well chosen cohesion markers are not present:
A conditional sentence structure contains the "if" portion of the statement, but no "then" portion leaving the sentence incomplete.

25b. Temporal ordering of ideas or elements is inaccurate:
Time information is omitted or ordered incorrectly.

25c. Transitional phrases are not used: The interpreter makes no difference between new ideas and ideas that have been concluded.

25d. Transitions are made with filler words: The interpreter says, "oh," "umm," or "you know" a lot.

25e. The same transitional phrase is used repeatedly: For example, the interpreter overuses the phrase "so then," as a sentence connector.

25f. The interpreter fails to signal a transition to an ending:
The interpreter's voice becomes louder instead of becoming softer.

Discussion

121

Cohesion markers permit the expression of complex ideas and relationships in a sentence, or between groups of sentences or throughout the entire text. They may be used to convey relationships of cause and effect, time, temporal ordering, spatial relationships, or to communicate the speaker's feelings or attitude toward the topic and/or toward the audience.

For the average non-deaf audience a certain amount of silence is considered part of comfortable communication. Every second does not have to be filled with sound or speech. At times, interpreters feel a need to eliminate silences by saying something, sometimes anything, to fill the void. Interpreters should try to avoid filling in all silences with unnecessary words. The audience needs time to digest the information they are hearing, and in most cases, silences accurately reflect the communication goals of the signer.

25a.   Well chosen cohesion markers are not present.

In English, prepositions like "on," "over," "with" and conjunctions, like "and" or "but," are used for cohesion and to make transitions between thoughts and ideas. Cohesion markers are found both at the sentence level and between sentences. The interpreter must aim for the most natural English expression possible when using cohesion markers. For example, in the statement, "The interpreter is here today only, and will not be here tomorrow" the best choice of conjunction would be "but" instead of "and."

25b.   Temporal ordering of ideas or elements is inaccurate.

Using transitions to convey temporal ordering is another way of providing cohesion. For example, "first," "second" and "third" are words that express the concept of "sequence" and the order of items in sequence. Conjunctive adverbs like "then" and "thereafter" serve a similar ordering function. For example the statement, "I went to the store and then to the vet," provides a sequence of events. The listener understands which was accomplished first and which second. In contrast, the statement "I went to the store and the vet," provides no explicit information about the order in which these two events occurred. If the signer specifies order, it should be retained in the interpretation. Other "connective" words and phrases like "previously," "at an earlier period," "formerly," "at the same moment," "during this time," "in the same period" and "throughout this period," are also useful to convey an order of events.

25c.   Transitional phrases are not used.

Transitional words and phrases are used to connect thoughts in varied ways. It is often appropriate to make a short sentence and start a new, linked sentence with a word or phrase such as "consequently," "as a result of," "in addition to," and "in conclusion." These transitions provide linkages between points and direct the audience's attention to what was said and what is going to be said next. For example, the interpreter might say, "Having described the problem, we can start to think about the solution." Using such elements well enables interpreters to provide a more fluid and coherent message in the target language. Joining everything by "and" does not indicate the completion of one thought and the introduction of another.

25d.   Transitions are made with filler words.

Filler words such as "oh," "um," "you know" and "kind of like" should be avoided in the interpretation. They add no meaning to the message. Instead, meaning can be altered because frequent use of fillers makes signers sound unsure and tentative to the audience.

Some fillers are extraneous and only appear to provide information. Filler phrases such as "in order to" and "because of the fact that" can often be shortened to "to" or "because" with no loss of clarity in meaning. Filler phrases such as "in a manner of speaking" and "for all intents and purposes" can often be deleted altogether.

123

Filler words should be used only when signers use fillers themselves; they should not be used as replacements for brief silences or when the interpreter is thinking of how to interpret a message. Fillers can cause the interpretation to sound too rapid because of the number of words they import into the work. Using them often means adding several words when a single word will do. When shorter, less "wordy" constructions are used, the interpretation will sound more natural, assuming this natural quality reflects the signer's intent.

25e.   The same transitional phrase is used repeatedly.

A variety of transitional words and phrases are available. Interpreters should vary their choices to avoid repetition and provide interest to the message. Commonly, overused terms stringing several sentences together include "and," "then" and "so." For example, "I was going to the vet. <u>So</u> I brought my dog in his cage. <u>So</u> the vet saw my dog and gave him his annual shots."

25f.   Interpreter fails to signal a transition to an ending.

Most interactions have some kind of beginning, middle and end. There are cultural expectations surrounding this structuring and packaging of communication. The beginning of utterances within a discourse must in some way gather or release an audience's attention. For example, in ASL the sign CURIOUS is used to open conversation. Other conversational openers include DOESN'T MATTER, FINE, KNOW-THAT, THEN, and time indicators. When ending in ASL there is repetition, pause, or a pace change. Physically in ASL the head is down, there is a decisive head nod, hands drop out of signing space or rest position, body shift and eye gaze change, and shoulders are down. These conventions let people know where they are in a discourse.

To signal an end or stopping point for an English speaking audience the voice is often slightly lowered, a pause is present, the pace is slower. Then, for the beginning of the next utterance, the voice is slightly louder. For closing a discussion or ending a talk, the voice becomes a little softer. The voice indicates that the conclusion is approaching. In the research samples, often the interpreters' voices became louder towards the end of their work. It appeared that interpreters were excited to get to the end of the text and therefore tended to speak louder. This reaction gave incongruent aural information to the audience, who understood the increasing "energy" in the voices to mean that there was more to be said.

26. **The interpretation flows (carries the audience) from the beginning of the discourse to the end. (See also Pace.)**

Possible errors

26a. The interpreter appears to be searching for the right lexical items and phrases to use: The interpreter starts a sentence about a head-on collision, but can't "find" the word "collision" and has to <u>restructure</u> the sentence to say, "two cars hit each other."

26b. The flow in the interpretation is uneven: The interpreter speaks too fast and falls into long pauses.

26c. There is a marked difference in the flow of different sections of the interpretation: The interpreter pauses awkwardly trying to get the gist of a new topic.

Discussion

One of the goals of discourse production is to control variations in the speed of delivery to help to convey the signer's intent. It is important for the message to flow well from one section to the next without unusual breaks or insertion of unusual lexical choices which add discordant information. Phrasing chosen by the interpreter is a key technique in making an interpretation flow. The phrasing used by an interpreter depends on the signer's intent and must retain the signer's perspective. As a rule of thumb, phrasing in blocks of six words or less, followed by a pause is comfortable for audiences. Using this rhythm, a breath can be taken during the pause.

26a.   The interpreter appears to be searching for the right lexical items and phrases to use.

At times the discourse produced may lack flow because an interpreter is searching for the right word or phrase to use. This is a recognized problem in interpretation, and there are some contributing factors that can be controlled. For example, it is important to avoid hunting up "50 cent words" or trying to work at the outer limits of ones vocabulary skills. Often, "just saying it" is the best practice. Obvious vocabulary searches draw the audience's attention to the interpreter and away from the signer. Of course, if signers have an unnatural flow or are awkward in their presentation manner, then interpreting with an awkward flow is not an error; it matches the signer's delivery style.

26b.   The flow in the interpretation is uneven.

Once flow in the interpretation is established, it should be consistent throughout the discourse. If flow changes, it should be because the signer's discourse changes. Usually, however, false starts (starting and stopping, and starting again) or an increase in pace, followed by longer than usual pauses reflect only a labored interpretation process. For example, "I drove and drove to get…so, I was driving the car and…" is a result of a false start.

26c.   There is a marked difference in the flow of different sections of the interpretation.

Often the research samples showed interpretations that flowed effectively in some sections, but not in others. Flow disruptions occurred most regularly when signers introduced new topics or used asides in their discourse. For example, the flow at the beginning of sections of discourse may be weak. Then, as the interpreter becomes confident about his or her skill in conveying content, the flow improves greatly. On occasion flow was lacking at the end of a long discourse (i.e., longer than 30 minutes). Fatigue can affect an interpreter's ability to sustain fluidity. There may also be a noticeable change in flow as an interpreter gets to the end of "rehearsed" sections or sections that an interpreter was able to discuss with a signer beforehand. This might happen, for example, if members of the audience ask unexpected questions.

NOTE: The more an interpreter knows the better. Background is important in order to make the best semantic choices. If the interpreter knows what happened in previous interactions, it is easier to provide an interpretation. This is especially true for on-going situations, such as staff meetings or any regular gathering where the participants are familiar with one another as well as with the content.

27. Emphasis appears appropriately in the interpretation.

Possible errors

27a. Emphasis is missing: The interpreter voices all words and phrases in the same tone.

27b. Emphasis is used in the wrong places: The interpreter highlights something the signer has not emphasized.

27c. Emphasis is overused: The interpreter stresses everything.

27d. Emphasis is used without variety: The interpreter repetitively chooses one way to convey emphasis, leaving no way to communicate relative degrees of emphasis in the signer's message.

Discussion

The meaning of a message can be changed by the manner in which something is said. English is a "stressed" language which is voiced with vocal variations. Interpreters can use this characteristic of the language to provide meaning in the interpreted message. For example, the meaning of the following simple sentence can be altered greatly by emphasizing a different word:

Trinka hates DOGS;

TRINKA hates dogs; and,
Trinka HATES dogs.

When the voice is used effectively, the significance of words can be altered. An analogy would be underlining and bolding words on the computer screen.

It is a common misconception that loudness is the best or only way to provide emphasis. However, once a message is comfortably audible, it is not only loudness that affects reception of a message. Reception and response are also affected, for instance, by clarity of enunciation. Words shouldn't be "pushed" for emphasis; they should be "lifted out." Loudness is not always the best way to "lift out" portions of text. In fact, dropping one's volume can have the same result.

27a. Emphasis is missing.

When emphasis is not provided in an interpretation, the entire discourse has the same meaning "weight." This lack of vocal variation is not natural for English speakers or listeners. Audiences are generally inattentive to a monotonous voice. In addition, this "flat" voice would very seldom accurately reflect a signer's intent, because no shades of meaning are conveyed.

27b. Emphasis is used in the wrong places.

When signers use emphasis, it should be reflected in emphatic moments in the interpretation. Words and phrases that convey high points in the signer's discourse in English should be "lifted out" by different voicing. The task is to understand and apply various emphasis options in English that match the signer's use of emphasis strategies in ASL. Interpreters must be careful not to over-emphasize certain words and phrases in a way that doesn't correspond to the signer's intent. For example, sometimes emphasis is needed on the small words that are often unstressed in English such as "a," "the" or "of." For example, the signer says DOG MOVE++ CAN'T, MUST FIND ONE. The interpreter might say, "my dog needs a place to stay" but to convey the signer's intent, should say, "my dog needs <u>a</u> place to stay" (i.e., not several places).

27c. Emphasis is overused.

The research samples also showed interpretations in which over-emphasis did not vary. No difference was conveyed between important points, less important points and unimportant points. From the listener's perspective continued overemphasis is tiresome. The signer can be "blamed" for the audience's own negative reactions.

27d. Emphasis is used without variety.

If only one strategy is used for emphasis, the interpreter is introducing redundancy that may not be present in the source message. Ideally, several strategies for emphasis should be utilized. For example, in addition to loudness, words can be stretched out, so they take longer to say than other words, they can be said softly, or the enunciation can be "clipped."

28. Repairs are made appropriately within the interpretation.

Possible errors

28a. Repairs are not made: Errors appear to go unnoticed.

28b. Apologies are added: The interpreter says, "I'm sorry. I missed that."

28c. Phrases are used that do not make sense to the audience: The interpreter says "I missed that fingerspelling" when the term "fingerspelling" doesn't make sense to the audience.

129

28d. Distinctions between a signer error and an interpreter error are not made clear: The interpreter says, "I don't mean running, I meant shooting," and does not preface the repair by saying, "the interpreter made an error."

28e. Errors are repaired excessively: The flow of discourse is damaged by frequent corrections.

28f. Extreme repairs are made for minor errors: The interpreter mispronounces a name and says, "Excuse me, interpreter error, it's not ... but...."

28g. Minimal repairs are made for serious errors: A few paragraphs are interpreted using the wrong referent, such as the city "Guadalajara." Later the interpreter determines that "Guadeloupe" was the correct city and starts using Guadeloupe, which is correct, but no repair was indicated in the interpretation.

Discussion

In all forms of communication it is common for errors to occur. Just as there are no hard and fast rules for error correction in speech, there are no strategies for interpreters that work in every situation. Some interpreters have a sense of how it sounds when they are making repairs. Others just do the best they can under the circumstances.

It is useful for interpreters to develop a few strategies, by reflecting on error situations encountered in work situations. Usually, naturalness is the key. The audience and the signer are disturbed as little as possible and the flow of the communication is retained.

Sometimes, it's hard to define an interpretation error. What really needs to be corrected, and what can be left in the interest of flow and the relative importance of other message components? When is the signer's help needed or useful?

Some deaf people have a sense of what they want to have happen when an interpretation error occurs. Some choose to stop the flow of their communication and have the interpreter do the repair. At other times, the deaf person wants to be told by the interpreter that there was an error and what it was. Then the deaf person can re-iterate and explain what was meant and explain the interpretation error. In this latter case, the deaf person takes on a significant responsibility for working with the non-deaf audience and the providing information about the success or lack of success in the interpretation.

Often the more specific interpreters can be as to the reason they are missing information, the easier it is for the audience to understand what is going on. The interpreter might say, for instance, "The signer is hidden from the interpreter's view." This lets the audience know that the signer has either moved off camera or perhaps is standing behind a podium, or someone is walking in front of the interpreter. The general phrase, "the interpreter missed some information," is not a very helpful addition. While the audience knows something is missed, they are left wondering how much or how significant the information loss may be.

It might be better to say, "The interpreter missed the name of the uncle." However, if the uncle's name is determined to be insignificant, the interpreter can choose to use a general pronoun, "he" instead of the exact name that was missed. This way of handling the error may even be a better alternative than announcing to the audience that the uncle's name was missed. It is often useful to save larger, more intrusive repairs for occasions when it is crucial to the message that the uncle's name be given.

Self-monitoring of a performance is required for achieving successful interpretation work. When errors are noticed, repairs are needed to achieve message equivalency. It is up to the interpreter to determine the most appropriate way to handle corrections at any given time. He or she must determine when there is an error, when it needs to be repaired, and how to repair it, while at the same time continuing the interpretation. Repairs require ability to "multi-task," so that none of the signer's information is missed.

At times the interpreter may not be able to interrupt the signer, to get information needed for a repair – for instance, if the presentation is on videotape. A number of solutions are possible in such cases. For example, the interpreter can say, "The interpreter is unsure of who was in the car accident, but believes it is the signer's wife." It is a better solution to somehow acknowledge there is confusion than to ignore it.

131

It would be incorrect to leave the audience believing that the interpretation was totally accurate.

When interpreters recognize an error and determine the best way to repair it, they can make the repair and move on. Interpreters should avoid obsessing about errors so that they don't lose focus on the interpretation task as a whole.

28a.   Repairs are not made.

It is important that interpreters monitor their own discourse to recognize and repair errors as they occur. When errors go unnoticed and are left to stand, they skew the message and leave the audience with inaccurate information.

28b.   Apologies are added.

The research samples contained many examples of interpreters, especially women, apologizing during their interpretation. This observation is consistent with the interactional role of "peacemaker" that women often take on in general conversation. However, apologies add words to the interpretation without improving message equivalency. In normal speech, native English speakers often mispronounce words and simply re-pronounce them accurately and keep going. They usually don't say, "I'm sorry, what I meant to say was…" The addition of the apology adds gravity to an error that may not be appropriate, especially in informal situations.

NOTE: This is not to say that apologies should never be used. If there is a serious error that really throws an audience off track, it is respectful to apologize. For instance, if the interpreter realizes that the topic of discourse is not motorcycling, but snowmobiling, an overt apology can be appropriate, and would not be an error.

28c. Phrases are used that do not make sense to the audience.

Sometimes interpreters must make the audience aware of missed information or a problem that occurred in the interpretation. If this is the case, phrases should be used that the audience understands, such as, "The interpreter has missed information about the way to tell the difference between an original and a counterfeit Canadian $20 bill." This kind of interjection lets the audience know that something is missing, and also what was missed. Simply saying, "the interpreter has missed some information," leaves the audience wondering what was omitted in the interpretation.

28d. Distinctions between a signer error and an interpreter error are not made clear.

In the interpretation it must be made clear when the interpreter has made an error so as to reduce negative audience perception of the signer's message. Taking ownership of errors involves making it clear to the audience that it is an interpretation error, and not the signer "mis-speaking." Sometimes signers make mistakes and rectify them. When this occurs, the interpretation reflects the error as it is signed and then the correction. It then comes across to the audience that it is the signer's error.

Often a repair can be postponed to a slightly later point in the interpretation. For example, towards the end of a story about two men, the interpreter might say, "It was not Bill it was Bob who did....." The manner in which the statement is voiced during the repair will let the audience know the interpreter is repairing an interpretation error not a signer error.

28e.   Errors are repaired excessively.

Errors vary in seriousness and may need to be treated differently when planning repairs. Not every error needs to be repaired. For instance, simply stumbling over words doesn't always call for a repair. If every little error is repaired, the target language message can become more awkward than if the errors had been left to stand.

28f.   Extreme repairs are made for minor errors.

Once an interpreter determines that a repair must be made, he or she must decide when to act. The resulting repair must be consistent with the gravity of the error. For example, for minor errors, it would be an overstatement to say, "Oh, that was wrong. It is 1989, not 1986." Simply changing the number to "1989" is sufficient. Another example might occur when an interpreter glosses ASL signs in error. He or she might then produce the proper English lexical choice. It would sound like "I 'touched', <u>visited</u> 12 countries. "Visited" is said with force but without overtly indicating it was a repair. However, this approach makes good auditory sense, and the listener will recognize the added word as a repair.

28g.   Minimal repairs are made for serious errors.

When more serious errors occur, the interpretation should include a thorough explanation of the problem. For example, if interpreting for a computer programmer, the discussion involves technical terms, the interpreter may interpret a particular word incorrectly for several paragraphs before realizing the error. It would then be appropriate to say something to the audience that clarifies what has happened. For example the interpreter might say, "The interpreter has been using the term internet, however the correct term is <u>intra</u>net, not <u>inter</u>net."

29. **The interpreter manages the interpretation process effectively.**
(See also Pace, Flow.)

Possible errors

29a. Interpretation follows too quickly after the production of the source message so there is insufficient processing time: The interpreter says, "When I was ten years old...when <u>my son</u> was ten."

29b. The interpreter inserts extended processing time, and the English discourse sounds unnatural: The interpretation sounds like, "I want...to know...."

29c. External processing occurs: The interpreter adds, "I think he is saying..." to the message.

29d. The interpreter fails to manage stressful elements of the interpretation process like handling new information or their own fatigue levels: More errors are present toward the end of the interpretation as the interpreter tires.

29e. The interpreter doesn't develop a structure for conveying main points: The signer has six main points but the interpretation is not set up to provide equal weight to all six.

29f. The details are interpreted inaccurately: Details in the interpretation seem extraneous.

Discussion

Interpretation is a difficult and challenging task. ASL is a visual-spatial language, and signs, non-manual features, and use of space all occur simultaneously. English, in contrast, conveys information sequentially. In effective interpretations this significant transition from one language structure to the other is invisible or "seamless" to the audience. To achieve this effect, interpreters need talent in producing natural sounding English discourse. They also need to be aware of pitfalls in the interpretation process and to develop strategies for managing language-to-language transitions.

29a. Interpretation follows too quickly after the production of the source message so there is insufficient processing time.

False starts were noted frequently in the research samples. They occurred at the beginning of sentence structures, often when the processing time, or lag time, was less than the time needed to produce a complete and accurate sentence. False starts occur when interpreters begin producing a sentence and then, shortly after, begin to realize that a repair is necessary or additional information must be communicated. The sentence is begun and then is restated, using a more appropriate sentence structure. For example, "we're going...we went to the public market" contains a false start which is followed by an accurate interpretation. In this instance the false start involved repair to the verb tense.

It is good practice to wait to truly understand the signer's idea before beginning the interpretation. However, the interpreter can start a sentence while still processing if a pause is becoming too long for audience comfort levels. For example, he or she may slowly say an introductory sentence to give him or herself time to get into the "meat" of the signer's message. This is a better strategy than starting too quickly and glossing ASL signs without any real grasp of the topic.

Another trouble spot is inaccurate anticipation of meaning. For example, the signer is describing the layout of a very large house. When she gets to the master bedroom, she says it is the "owner's bedroom" which is what she really meant, but the interpreter assumes she means the "master bedroom." The fact is that the owner of the house lives in one bedroom and rents two rooms, including the master bedroom.

29b. **The interpreter inserts extended processing time, and the English discourse sounds unnatural.**

The overall pacing of delivery of the English interpretation must be comfortable for the audience if the signer's message is to be comprehended. For example, it is unusual in English to have long silences. If they occur in the interpretation, the audience can become uncomfortable, and begin to lack confidence in the interpretation and/or the signer.

29c. **External processing occurs.**

On occasion the research samples showed evidence of external processing. In some cases, interpreters articulated out loud what they were thinking, such as "This isn't making any sense," or "Do you know what I mean?" Interpreters also actually voiced their personal reactions to the signer's message or to their own work. For example, when interpreters were unsure of the source language message, they said things such as, "I think he means that...(meaning the signer)." Sometimes, interpreters said "damn" or some other swear word in reaction to an error of their own. Other vocalizations noted in the research samples included statements such as "Oh!" or "Now I understand!" indicating that the interpreter suddenly grasped the information and/or is surprised. These vocal expressions are inappropriate and must not be used in the interpretation. In general, interpreters should mask their own feelings but not the signer's feelings.

Sometimes interpreters may find themselves needing the audience to fill in some content they can not handle, like the pronunciation of a foreign name. In such cases, interpreters may choose to use a general phrase like "this man" or "my friend" and not attempt an unfamiliar name. Or, they can make a stab at the pronunciation and at least provide the audience with some information about the name of the person.

137

29d. **The interpreter fails to manage stressful elements of the interpretation process like handling new information or their own fatigue levels.**

It is often difficult to be consistently accurate throughout an interpretation. Some portions of the interpretation may be very accurate, whereas in other sections errors may be present. It is important to note the areas where errors are most prevalent to look for patterns of inconsistency in the accuracy of the interpretation. For example, comprehension of ASL, unlike English, requires the use of eye muscles. If eye fatigue occurs, the interpretation may be less successful or less accurate from the middle to end of the interpretation.

29e. **The interpreter doesn't develop a structure for conveying main points.**

The main points in the discourse must all be interpreted accurately. For example, if the signer has six points, the interpretation might stress that content organization. "I want to make six points. First… Second…." It would be an error if the signer has three points and two examples of the second point, and the interpreter makes the second example a separate main point.

29f. **The details are interpreted inaccurately.**

Details provide flavor to a message and are an important support to the main ideas of the discourse. Sentence structure must be chosen to
accommodate all important information, and details must be incorporated so that they support or illustrate main points in the signer's message. For example, the signer provides information about cooking a soufflé and relates each detail about the process to the dining experience. The interpretation mentions greasing the soufflé

dish but doesn't link the information to serving the soufflé successfully. In this case, details are provided but some of the main point is lost.

Interpreters must also recognize details in the signer's message which should not be conveyed to the audience. For example, sometimes a signer repeats something, like fingerspelling to help the interpreters out. This information is not intended for the audience.

Delivery: Public Speaking

OVERVIEW

The focus of assessment in this section is the skills needed to deliver a spoken English message. Education for interpreters tends to focus primarily on message content rather than message delivery, although skilled public speaking is crucial in providing effective interpretations. Skills such as choosing effective pitch, pace, pauses, and projection are vital for conveying meaning to an audience. Research consistently finds that audiences develop an impression of speakers less from *what* they say, than from *how* they say it. Voice and non-verbal communication are central, while the words themselves account for a relatively insignificant amount of the total message. It is clear that the manner in which a message is delivered is a critical element in providing equivalency to the signer's message.

Because English is an oral/aural language, patterns of phrasing and intonation help the audience to comprehend the tone and meaning of a signer's message. Variations of "voicing" must carry all the information and nuance expressed by the signer's "visual" discourse.

Breathing control is a key aspect of being able to take advantage of the vocal richness available in spoken languages. That is why actors, for instance, take voice or elocution classes. They learn control techniques for all the muscle groups – from diaphragm to tongue – which are involved in speaking. Fine tuning these techniques allows a speaker to produce a range of effects on an audience, like calming them or inspiring them.

| 30. | **Breathing is controlled while interpreting.** |

Possible errors

30a. Breathiness is audible: All words are spoken with too much air.

30b. Outbursts of breath are audible: The interpreter exhales loudly.

30c. Taking in breath is audible: The interpreter sucks in air noisily, perhaps by mouth breathing.

30d. Breath is taken at inappropriate places: The interpreter needs air in the middle of phrases causing unnatural pausing/phrasing.

Discussion

The difference between breathing to take in oxygen and breathing as part of vocal technique while speaking is significant. For instance, natural breathing is rhythmic, but when speaking breathing is not evenly paced; breath is taken in quickly and exhaled slowly in a controlled way to articulate meaningful sounds. The rhythm for exhaling depends on what is being said. Breath is often taken in quickly during a pause between ideas, replenishing air that has been expelled.

Although breathing is controlled in these ways while speaking the effect is to produce "natural sounding" speech. Breath is controlled by:
o   the diaphragm muscle situated in the area below the lungs and above the waist;
o   the abdominal muscles circling the waist; and,
o   the intercostal muscles that raise and lower the ribs. Lungs must fill completely to use these three muscle groups effectively in controlling exhalation for clear, expressive speech.

Good diaphragm control enables a speaker to project his or her voice across a distance. In its role as the main breathing muscle, the diaphragm is used to fill the lower part of the lungs to provide enough air for timed, controlled exhalation. The interpreter then has a great deal of flexibility in phrasing and expression because there is no pressing need for air. To improve breath intake ribs can be lifted, the diaphragm can be pushed down, and the abdominal muscles around the waist can also be used. The lungs although comfortably filled, should not be "bursting" with air. With proper lung inflation sounds are emitted with controlled force. Using breath from deep in the lungs makes the sound powerful and full. Most importantly, full sound is produced without strain to the vocal cords.

Posture also affects breathing. Tilting the head up and/or down can affect the *trachea*, the breathing channel. The best posture is to look straight ahead. Shallow breathing, or using only air from the upper part of the lungs, causes production to sound forced and inflexible. Interpreters need to speak *through* their throat and not *push* their message out with their throat. Fatigue occurs when squeezing words out with the throat muscles and increasing vocal chord tension. Voice quality can deteriorate during the interpretation because of this "pushing." The voice can become raspy or sound like shouting when this is not the signer's intent. Air should be expelled by using the diaphragm with controlled force and not by "squeezing" out the voice.

30a.   Breathiness is audible.

"Breathiness" can be a problem when speaking in quiet tones and sometimes occurs when speaking pace is too fast for comfortable, natural breath intake. The speaker then sounds rushed, and breathing sounds are audible. Sometimes, breathiness can even make words difficult for an audience to pickup. For instance, if the speaker says, "ta<u>b</u>" and ends with a breathy exhalation instead of closed lips, the audience might hear "ta<u>p</u>." "P" as an unvoiced consonant is distinguishable by an "out" breath as it is sounded.

Exaggerated tonal qualities, like "breathiness," impose the interpreter's personality on the information being communicated. For example, if the signer is a doctor talking about cancer and cancer's side effects on the body, a breathy voice would be incongruent with the seriousness of the situation. A breathy delivery would have an almost "gossipy" tone.

30b.   Outbursts of breath are audible.

Uncontrolled outbursts of air should be avoided. In most situations, the audience should be completely unaware of how the interpreter is breathing. An exception would be if the signer's intent includes dramatic breathing or exasperated sighs.

30c.   Taking in breath is audible.

Inhalation should also be quiet. Audible intakes of air carry a meaning for an audience which is clearly not present in the signer's message. The audience may think that the signer is "surprised," or "tired" or "nervous." English speakers pick up a range of "messages" from "extra" breathing sounds made by someone who is talking.

30d.   Breath is taken at inappropriate places.

Breath should be taken in during natural pauses in the spoken discourse, and these necessary inhalations should also be silent. Often only a small intake is needed to replace the bit of air that has just been expelled. Air intake and exhalations can easily be achieved during short pauses in the interpretation.

31.   The interpreter's voice projection is appropriate for the setting.

Possible errors

31a. The projection is too weak: The interpreter can't be heard at the back of the room.

31b. The volume is too loud or too soft: The loudness of the message is overwhelming.

31c. The voice intensity lacks variety: The interpreter's delivery is monotonous.

31d. The volume fades away: The interpreter is out of breath at the end of sentences.

Discussion

Projection and volume refer to the force of the voice. Every person in the audience should be able to hear the interpretation without straining. Sound must be projected up from the diaphragm through the vocal cords. The mouth and jaw must be relaxed and open to produce tone and clarity. The interpreter should speak with energy.

The energy level in the interpreter's voice must correspond with the energy conveyed by the signer.

31a.   The projection is too weak.

If the voice projection is weak, then speech is likely to be too quiet to be heard easily. It may seem to the audience that the signer is reluctant to communicate if the interpreter's projection is weak or hesitant.

31b.   The volume is too loud or too soft.

If the volume of the voicing is too soft or too loud, the signer may be perceived to be insensitive to the surroundings and/or the audience. For example, using an overpowering voice to talk about how to wash and change a baby would be incongruent. The audience would feel as though the signer was brusque or insensitive to babies. Loud interpretations can also come across as brash or autocratic in some situations. The audience may have the unpleasant impression they are being yelled at.

When the signer raises major points the volume should be strengthened. However, lowering the voice can also cause the audience to take special note of the message. Speaking that is constantly loud or constantly soft sounds unnatural. It results in an uninteresting and monotonous interpretation that loses the audience's attention. One should increase or decrease volume to introduce or emphasize new points. The volume, along with voice projection, can be slightly louder and stronger in parts of the interpretation and then return to the neutral speech level. Volume control errors can be caused by premature focus on the next sentence. When this happens, the interpreter may forget to complete the previous sentence with an appropriate volume. *147*

31c.   The voice intensity lacks variety.

Variety in voice projection is a big part of successful and effective interpretations. The intensity with which speech is voiced is very important in conveying shades of emotion and commitment. Intensity is not the same as loudness – it refers to a controlled energy the speaker uses in communicating. For example, whispering can be used very effectively to express the importance of a message – often more effectively than shouting. One can also speak quietly and with purpose. Varying intensity well is an attention grabber and should be used as a communication tool in most interpretations.

31d.   The volume fades away.

The research material often showed that interpreters' projection faded away at inopportune times during the interpretation. For example, when coming to an important point, the interpreters seemed to run out of breath causing that section of the message to fade out instead of becoming louder and clearer to make the point evident.

32.   Pausing is used effectively in the interpretation to convey concise and clear meaning. (See also Flow.)

Possible errors

32a. Pauses are not present in the interpretation:
The interpreter produces continuous babble.

32b. Pauses are present at awkward moments: The flow of discourse is interrupted in the middle of phrases.

32c. Pauses are uncomfortably long: Audiences are left wondering what is wrong.

Discussion

In interpretations, pauses of one or two seconds are appropriate between voiced ideas, assuming the signer is signing with pauses as well. These little silences provide time for the audience to digest incoming information. They also give interpreters time to process incoming information and to develop appropriate syntax and phrasing essential to articulate pieces of work. Pauses are also used to provide emphasis to particular elements of a discourse. They can be very dramatic.

32a. **Pauses are not present in the interpretation.**

Interpreters should not cut out normal pauses to fit more words in. If appropriate pauses are not present, the interpretation rambles and listeners have a difficult time digesting the signer's message.

32b. **Pauses are present at awkward moments.**

Pauses should be present before and/or after important words. A silence after important ideas lends gravity to the points made and allows an audience time to consider information more carefully. The task for the interpreter is to use pauses at natural break points in English. Awkwardness occurs sometimes because pausing is different between ASL and English. For example a signer would sign #CAR MY, BLUE with a pause after MY. The English interpretation "My car is blue" would have no pause. When pauses are inserted at inopportune times into the English interpretation, the message is disjointed, and the audience may miss the introduction of new ideas and important points.

32c. **Pauses are uncomfortably long.**

English speaking audiences pick up information from pauses that makes them feel either comfortable or uncomfortable about an interaction. Long breaks may convey the hidden message, "Something is wrong." It is important for interpreters to be aware that an audience is monitoring these "interaction" clues and not to leave listeners "hanging." Unexpectedly long pauses tend to make listeners anxious or impatient.

33. **The pace of the interpretation matches the pace of the signer and the setting.**

Possible errors

33a. The pace is too fast: Phrases or ideas are run together.
33b. The pace is too slow: The discourse lacks energy and interest.
33c. The pace is uneven: Quick tempo is interspersed with long pauses.
33d. The pace has limited variation: The discourse sounds monotonous.
33e. The pace does not match the signer's pace: The signer is excited and the interpretation is slow and relaxed.

Discussion

"Pace" is the rate of speech production. It depends on the time it takes to say words and phrases and to pause appropriately. On average, North Americans speak at 145-165 words per minute. Interpreters need to be aware of the overall pace of the interpretation and the time it takes to utter each word or series of words.

Pacing must be chosen that will permit an audience to understand the words and the meaning of the message and have time to integrate the information. It should also reflect how signers feel about the message they are delivering. A deliberate focused delivery often indicates a serious presentation. Interpreters can control the pace of discourse by varying the length of their pauses. For instance, if the signer is emphasizing an idea, the interpreter might say a word or phrase slowly, and follow that slow section with a slightly longer pause. In this way the signer's intent is captured and the audience gets time to absorb the signer's emphasis. The next sentence could then be followed by a shorter pause, so the interpreter can keep up with the signer.

33a.   The pace is too fast.

Speaking too rapidly makes it difficult for the audience to understand the interpretation. For example, it is difficult to hear auctioneers because of their very rapid speed; the audience should not be given the impression that the interpreter wants to get the information out quickly before it is forgotten; or that the interpreter is impatient or anxious to be finished. A fast pace should be used only if the signer intends to convey urgency or enthusiasm; pauses should still be inserted between each idea or phrase even if the pace is intentionally fast.

33b.   The pace is too slow.

If the pace of the interpretation is slow and yet the signer is visibly excited, the non-deaf audience would note the incongruity and wonder about the quality and accuracy of the interpretation.

33c.   The pace is uneven.

Speaking quickly but then using long pauses causes the message to sound disjointed. This pacing rushes the audience and then leaves them waiting. When the signer is controlled and deliberate but the pace of the interpretation is uneven in this "start-and-stop" way, message content is lost. The signer's sincerity, carefulness and clarity are not conveyed.

151

Sometimes interpreters have a tendency to go fast in the sections that they understand well and go slowly in sections where they are lost or unsure. There is also a temptation to speed up at the end of a lecture to "get it done."

33d.   The pace has limited variation.

Changing the pace of delivery, allows an interpreter to be a more effective speaker. For example, if it is necessary to regain the audience's attention, pace can be slowed down. The variation in pace, will "pick up" or "gather" an audience and cause listeners to pay closer attention. Pace changes can be effectively used to emphasize important points, or new points that the signer wants to introduce. In contrast, when the pace of the interpretation is unchanging, the audience is put to sleep.

33e.   The pace does not match the signer's pace.

Although ASL/English interpreters have a rate of production that is personally comfortable for them, it is important to put the priority on using a pace that matches the intent of the signer. For example, message equivalency is reduced if the interpretation is fast paced, but the signer is describing something in a slow and methodical manner. Discrepancy in pace is considered an error.

34.   The pitch of the voice is varied and natural (e.g., comfortable for the listeners). (See also Cohesion markers.)

Possible errors

34a. The pitch is very high: The interpreter sounds like a "nail on glass."

34b. The pitch is very low; The interpreter sounds stand-offish or sexy.

34c. Pitch changes for no apparent reason: The pitch goes up on insignificant words or phrases.

34d. The pitch is unchanging: Pitch is not used to signal new ideas or text breaks.

Discussion

Pitch, or vocal inflection, is what makes a voice interesting, alive and distinctive. Pitch depends on the frequency of sound waves created by air passing over the vocal cords – the higher the frequency, the higher a voice sounds. The average speaker has a vocal range of at least two octaves although people settle on a much narrower range in their ordinary speaking voices. Interpreters can learn to control or change their "natural" pitch. Some public speakers do so to project a particular image of themselves to their audience – calm, powerful or authoritative.

Tone of voice is used by interpreters to depict the facial and body communication of the signer. When the signer changes expression, the interpretation can reflect the change by varying the pitch of the spoken message appropriately. For example the signer's intent to convey a moment of understanding can be approximated by moving the voice through a pitch range within one word, such as "oooOOOooh." Interpreters must be aware that inflection can subtly change the meaning of the signer's message. It can add sarcasm, curiosity, or impatience to the message an audience gets.

Cadence is rhythmic rising and falling in the pitch of the voice. Sometimes it is used for artistic effect. For instance, most people recognize the emotions produced by singer/songwriter Bob Dylan's almost hypnotic use of cadence. Lack of cadence also delivers a clear if unpleasant message. An example would be the unrelenting "gabble" of hard-sell advertisements.

34a.   The pitch is very high.

Unnaturally high-pitched inflection is produced by tight vocal cords. Often pitch is high at the beginning of presentations because the interpreter is nervous. A high pitch also conveys excitement and may mean the signer is engaged by his or her topic. If this is what the signer intends, high pitch is appropriate and conveys an accurate message. However if pitch is communicating nervousness on the part of the interpreter, and not the signer, then it is an error. High pitch can be irritating to an audience and therefore distracting.

34b.   The pitch is very low.

Unnaturally low pitch can be equally distracting to the audience, and hard to hear. Low-pitched interpretations can come across as conveying indifference or secrecy which may not be part of the signer's message.

34c.   Pitch changes for no apparent reason.

Words or phrases voiced at the upper and lower ends of the pitch range are emphasized and draw an audience's attention. Interpreters should ensure that these heavily inflected parts of the discourse are key words or phrases, not words that hold little or no meaning, such as articles (e.g., "the," "an"). Emphasizing such words would surprise and confuse an audience, and if that is not the signer's intent, it would be an error.

A rising pitch suggests an incomplete or weak thought. It is a common error to raise pitch at the end of sentences, making every assertion a question. This use of pitch conveys lack of maturity in the speaker and an inappropriate need to solicit an audience's agreement, or to win acceptance on a personal level. A falling inflection completes the thought. It suggests certainty and control. Pitch should fall at the end of phrases and sentences.

154 34d.   The pitch is unchanging.

Most people use only two or three notes, a narrow range of pitch, in their conversational speech. This can be dull, monotonous, and uninspiring in public speaking when the audience has to listen for a long time. An interpreter's pitch should change every time a new idea is presented, to hold an audience's attention. A proficient speaker uses over a dozen pitches naturally and with ease. In contrast, a speaker with a lazy voice uses no vocal variety. He or she often conveys boredom, depression, fatigue or disinterest to an audience.

NOTE: Often projection, pitch and volume vary together. For example, when the pitch is raised, the volume can become stronger and when the pitch is lowered, the volume can drop, but should still be easily audible.

35. Words are articulated clearly and accurately.

Possible errors

35a. Articulation is inconsistent: The interpreter speaks more clearly in some sections than in others.
35b. The interpreter mumbles: The interpreter's speech is unclear.
35c. The voicing is nasal: Sounds are projected through the nose rather than the mouth.
35d. Full vowel or consonant sounds are omitted or added: The interpreter says, "want" instead of "won't." The interpreter fails to sound a consonant like "c" so "picture" becomes "pitcher."
35e. Words are mispronounced: The interpreter says, "zed" instead of "zee" to an American audience.

Discussion

Articulation, or enunciation, refers to the formation and sounding of words. Each syllable of each word should be clearly and crisply produced throughout the interpretation.

Problems of clarity often arise because body tension is transferred to the voice. If interpreters tighten the muscles in the jaw, neck or upper torso, this will affect the sound of the message. "Tight" delivery includes locking the jaw, and/or tightening the lips, tongue or throat.

The lower jaw should be loose, so that there is a space between the upper and back molars. Teeth should not be clenched or held tightly together.

35a.   Articulation is inconsistent.

Articulation may be inconsistent within an interpretation causing the overall message to be unclear. One common example is vocal "drop-offs." This term refers to a failure to articulate words or longer sections of the discourse completely. For example, the interpreter may hurry the articulation of some words and say, "I am going to come getcha." Or, sentences at the beginning of paragraphs may be more clearly articulated than those at the end.

35b.   The interpreter mumbles.

Mumbling is a problem caused by poor articulation at the front of the mouth. If the mouth does not move with energy, especially the lips and the jaw, the resulting sound is often muffled and words are slurred. The tongue moves over 200 times during every minute of speech and tongue usage is another important factor in clear articulation. Nervousness often causes mumbling because an interpreter who feels strain may tighten the muscles of the mouth and jaw.

35c.   The voicing is nasal.

The only nasalized sounds in English are "n," "ng" and "m." All other sounds are projected through the mouth. If the jaw is clenched, many sounds will come out the nose giving the message a nasal quality. If this occurs, the resulting message can sound whiney, unhappy or unsure.

35d. Full vowel or consonant sounds are omitted or added.

Clear articulation requires the use of full vowel sounds, and the sounding of all voiced or aspirated consonants. For example, correct articulation of "which" should sound different from "witch." The "h" is breathed or "aspirated" to distinguish the two words. Active articulation adds color and meaning to the message. For example, when reading "Little Red Riding Hood" out loud, the speaker might enunciate "all the better to eat you with" very slowly and clearly to bring the character of the big bad wolf to life.

35e. Words are mispronounced.

Pronunciation varies from region to region and regional differences must be taken into account. The most important consideration is to make sure the audience easily understands the message. For example, Canadians pronounce the letter "z" as "zed," whereas people from the United States often pronounce it "zee." Interpreters should follow the audience's usage whenever possible. When providing interpretations across borders, whether between two countries, or across informal regional divisions like those between the northern and southern parts of many states, interpreters should be aware of variations in pronunciation of words. They can then avoid confusing the audience or hampering their ability to understand the message easily.

For example, there are at least two acceptable ways to pronounce each of the following words: "tomato," "creek" and "garage." As long as the audience can easily understand the pronunciation of individual lexical items, using a particular pronunciation has little effect on the message. If pronunciation may be a factor in the audience's comprehension of the message, interpreters should choose the first pronunciation listed in the dictionary whenever possible.

Multi-syllabic words such as "impenetrable," technical terms, or unfamiliar or borrowed terms such as "lanai" (meaning "balcony" in

Hawaii and on the west coast of Canada and the United States) and "Miguel" (popular name for males in Spanish-speaking communities) may cause interpreters difficulty.

NOTE: With very few exceptions interpreters should not try to imitate accents. An interpreter could simply say, "the woman replied with a French accent and said..." or "With a southern twang the young boy said, 'Excuse me sir,'" rather than "performing" the differences. If interpreters change accent for a section of text, the audiences become interested in their "acting" instead of the signer's message and intent.

Composure and Appearance

OVERVIEW

Composure and appearance directly affect the success of an
interpretation. They are an important element of the interpreting
process even though at first, they seem to be rather insignificant.
Interpreters may feel that if they convey a message accurately and
eloquently, their appearance is of little consequence. However, this is
not the case. Both the audience and the signer are very much aware of
an interpreter's presence. Maintaining "composure" really means that
interpreters do not insert themselves, their personalities or any
problems that come up in the interpretation into the target message.

Videotapes of interpretation work are particularly useful in assessing
an interpreter's composure and appearance. Although, interpretation is
often done "live," taped work should be reviewed to find patterns of
presentation behavior. These might be missed in a one-time
assessment. Even if composure and appearance issues are not obvious
to an evaluator on a single run through, they still have an impact on
an audience. (See also Interpretation process.)

NOTE: If interpreters only introduce themselves on videotape and for
the rest of the tape only the signer is visible, then some of the skills in
this section can not be assessed.

36. **The interpreter makes no unnecessary sounds
while interpreting.**

Possible errors

36a. The interpreter reacts to the source message before
interpreting it: The interpreter laughs before completing
the interpretation of a joke.

36b. The interpreter's voice quality conveys meaning that is not
in the signer's message: The interpreter sounds nervous,
puzzled, or confused.

36c. The interpreter has distracting audible habits:
The interpreter sniffs or coughs.

Discussion

Interpreters must pay attention to unintended sounds or noises they make. The information audibly conveyed should be that of the signer only and not extraneous information arising from an interpreter's lack of composure.

36a.   The interpreter reacts to the source message before interpreting it.

The source message always takes precedence over any of the interpreter's personal reactions, such as laughing at a joke from the signer. On occasion, the research samples showed interpreters who laughed before interpreting the joke, causing the audience to wonder what was so funny. When the joke was finally relayed, it was not as funny. In switching momentarily from "interpreter" to "audience," the interpreter adversely affected the audience's reception of the signer's message.

36b.   The interpreter's voice quality conveys meaning that is not in the signer's message.

Although it may be difficult for interpreters to control their nerves, and therefore their voice quality, it is considered an error if the voice conveys meaning that the signer does not intend. For example, if the interpreter conveys nervousness through a quavering voice, the audience may assume the <u>signer</u> is nervous. Also, if the interpreter conveys puzzlement about the interpretation, the audience is left with the impression that the signer is puzzled or unsure of the content she or he is delivering. From an ethical point of view, it is important for interpreters to "own" their mistakes and uncertainty. That means making the effort not to let the audience think it is the signer who is unsure. (See also Repairs.)

36c.   The interpreter has distracting audible habits.

Habits that are audible to the audience like biting one's nails, sighing, smacking one's lips or clearing one's throat should also be avoided. All of these extraneous noises in the interpretation are incongruent with the message.

37. The interpreter's expression fits the setting.

Possible errors

37a. Facial expression is frozen: The interpreter tries to maintain the perfect smile.

37b. Facial expression is blank: The interpreter keeps a "deadpan" face.

37c. Facial expression shows distracting emotion: The interpreter frowns in a puzzled way.

37d. The interpreter's own attitude is visibly expressed: The interpreter's face shows dislike or approval.

Discussion

Interpreters must be much more aware of their facial expressions when interpreting, than they need to be in ordinary speech. Many deaf people are very sensitive to interpreters' expressions. The objective, therefore, is to have a facial expression that is professional, pleasant and neutral. Expressions should be congruent with the context. It would be inappropriate, for example, to look somber while interpreting for a humorous signer.

37a.   Facial expression is frozen.
37b.   Facial expression is blank.

The face should express that the interpreter is relaxed and

comfortable. It is important to avoid a frozen look, or an expressionless face (e.g., a stone face or poker face). Facial expression that does not reflect the source message should be avoided.

37c.   Facial expression shows distracting emotion.

Grimaces or quizzical expressions, that for English speakers are normal when concentrating, can be confusing to a signer. It may appear that the interpreter does not understand the message. A quizzical expression should only be used when there is serious confusion and the interpreter really does need to ask for clarification.

NOTE: Showing confusion exclusively with facial expression is often not an effective way to communicate because it is not clear what exactly is "puzzling" the interpreter. It leaves the signer with the responsibility to figure out <u>what</u> is wrong. It is preferable for the interpreter to use a hand wave to get the deaf person's attention and/or to repeat a sign or signs that the interpreter did not understand. Then, the deaf person can go back to the appropriate place in his or her speech to clear up the confusion.

37d.   The interpreter's own attitude is visibly expressed.

The interpreter's attitude and train of thought is visible in a variety of ways to anyone watching. Interpreters may respond facially to their specific slip-ups. For instance, they might roll their eyes after mispronouncing a word. Signers can misunderstand interpreters' expressions as a response to the signer's own performance. Interpreters need to learn not to communicate their feelings about the success of their own effort to those watching. If the face shows unhappiness, the message will also, often <u>sound</u> unhappy. You can, in other words, "hear" a smile <u>and</u> the lack of one. If the facial expression is open and smiling, the voiced message will convey that attitude to listeners.

It is never appropriate for interpreter bias to intrude into the discourse through unconscious facial expressions. This holds true even if the interpreter finds the signer's topic unpleasant or revolting. Displaying superiority or aloofness puts the interpreter in a negative light. Skill in controlling this natural response to the stress of public speaking and interpreting, is an element of professionalism.

NOTE: If information relayed by a signer is inaccurate, the interpreter must relay this content in the same manner as the rest of the interpretation. For example, a signer might be explaining, "Beer is prevalent in Germany because all Germans are alcoholics." The interpreter's own beliefs and perspectives about beer or about people of German nationality can not be added to "correct" this content.

38. **Good eye contact is maintained with the signer.**

Possible errors

38a. The interpreter stares at the signer: The interpreter's gaze is unblinking and intense.

38b. The interpreter's eye gaze wanders excessively away from the signer: The interpreter scans the room absent-mindedly when thinking of how to say something.

38c. The interpreter watches the signer's hands instead of his or her face.

Discussion

Eye contact is an important element of communication. This is especially true when using a visual language. For one thing, the interpreter must watch the signer carefully enough to see the entire signed message. For another, the interpreter's regard must be comfortable for the person being looked at. The signer should not feel there is a staring contest going on, nor that the interpreter is uncomfortable and glancing away constantly in an embarrassed way.

38a.   The interpreter stares at the signer.

Eye contact maintained with the signer should be natural. Overdoing eye contact, or watching too intently makes an interpreter seem nervous or unsure. The signer may worry that the interpreter is not comprehending the message.

38b.   The interpreter's eye gaze wanders excessively away from the signer.

At times, the interpreter may look away from the signer, particularly if thinking about how to say something. Or the interpreter's eyes may close in concentration when trying to render the interpretation. Both of these "natural" behaviors cause interpreters to miss parts of the signer's message and therefore must be avoided. While interpreters may have a natural eye shift away from the signer when trying to retrieve a lexical item, this "introspection," literally "looking inward," should be kept to a minimum.

If there is insufficient eye contact, the signer can't get the interpreter's attention. When the signer realizes the interpreter has a tendency to look away, the signer may watch the interpreter more closely, suspecting some of the information is being omitted. This may distract the signer who should be free to concentrate on the audience and the presentation.

Interpreters sometimes try to <u>control</u> the flow and the speed of the signer's signing through avoiding eye contact. Unless the signer and the interpreter have agreed upon this tactic together, manipulating the signer in this manner is unethical and should be avoided. It conveys the same kind of aggression as deliberately looking away from a person who is talking to you in English. A more effective way of working is for interpreters to communicate directly with a signer to indicate their needs either before or during the presentation.

38c.   The interpreter watches the signer's hands instead of his or her face.

A common finding in the research samples was a tendency for interpreters to watch the signer's hands to follow the movements of signs or fingerspelling. Instead, it is important to focus on the face and use peripheral vision to comprehend the signs and fingerspelling. Watching the signer's hands every time a word is fingerspelled, is an ineffective way to capture information and is also very tiring for the eye muscles. This error is found most commonly among novice interpreters.

39.   Good posture is maintained throughout the interpretation.

Possible errors

39a. The interpreter slouches: The interpreter appears too relaxed.

39b. Posture is excessively erect: The interpreter looks stiff or uptight.

39c. The interpreter leans forward excessively: The interpreter wants a closer look at the signer, or is nervous.

Discussion

The body should be in a relaxed but erect position throughout an interpretation. Although, position can be changed during an interpretation and can vary throughout the work, changes are usually made at natural breaks in the signer's presentation, not during tense or emotional moments.

39a.   The interpreter slouches.

When interpreters become too comfortable, they may relax too much. For example, the shoulders may lean forward causing the chin to be held up and causing unnecessary strain on the interpreter's neck. This hunching can affect voice production. Or, the interpreter may sink low in a chair which looks unprofessional and restricts diaphragm control.

39b.   Posture is excessively erect.

Good posture should not be confused with rigid posture. The posture should communicate that an interpreter is relaxed and comfortable. Rigidity sends its own body language message to the audience, but also causes fatigue. When tired, an interpreter tends to loose focus and makes more errors of every kind.

39c.   The interpreter leans forward excessively.

The super-erect interpreter or one who is leaning forward appears nervous. This posture can actually cause the signer to become nervous and may skew the signer's own communication. The appearance of nervousness can also negatively affect the relationship between the signer and the audience. The audience gets uncomfortable or anxious and starts focusing on the interpreter more than on the message. It is imperative to maintain good but inconspicuous posture.

40.   The hands and body of the interpreter are held relatively still.

Possible errors

40a. The interpreter makes repetitive movements: The interpreter swivels a chair from side to side or taps a foot on the floor.

40b. There is excessive arm movement: The interpreter crosses and uncrosses his or her arms.

40c. The interpreter's hands copy the signer's signs: The interpreter mimics unfamiliar signs.

40d. Gestures are distracting: Interpreters twiddle thumbs, flail hands in search of the right words, or play with their hair.

40e. Head movements are inappropriate: The interpreter moves his or her head from left to right, looking like "no," but meaning an emphatic "yes."

Discussion

Physical movement in ASL is precise and deliberate because it is a visual language. When interpreters are trying to produce a verbal interpretation that is equivalent to the signer's message, they must keep two things in mind. First, their body language should conform to expectations of their English speaking audience. Second, their body language should be as calm as possible so as not to distract the signer with incongruent physical communication signals. Deaf people have mentioned that sharp, sudden movements sometimes cause the deaf person to think that the interpreter was stung by a bee or was hit from behind by someone in the audience. To avoid distracting the signer or the audience, interpreters must become aware of their own mannerisms and learn to control them.

Interpreters are often seated while interpreting from ASL to English. While seated, certain movements like crossing and uncrossing legs are natural ways to adjust positioning. However, if these movements occur repeatedly in a very short period of time, they become obtrusive and the interpreter calls attention to him or herself. The audience may feel the interpreter wishes to "interrupt," as fidgeting often signals a desire to speak in turn-taking behavior of English speakers.

The sitting position chosen is important. When a position is not comfortable for the interpreter, he or she is forced to maneuver into a more comfortable position or to a better location to see the signing more clearly. These movements may be distracting to the audience or signer. Good "sight lines" are an important element in choosing, before an interpretation starts, how and where to sit.

40a.   The interpreter makes repetitive movements.

Movements such as swinging back and forth in a movable chair or making rapid fidgeting movements of feet or legs can be very distracting to both the signer and the audience. Signers should be able to relax about the interpretation process and focus primarily on their message and its delivery to the audience. Interpreters need to acquire the "stillness" element of composure, so that they can use their bodies only for appropriate body language support of their target language message. If standing, interpreters should not move around as if giving a lecture.

———— 📖 ————

40b.   There is excessive arm movement.

While speaking, hands should be held in the lap to avoid distracting the signer. In some cases hand movement is used intentionally to attract a signer's attention. For example, an interpreter may repeat a sign or try to reiterate a fingerspelled word. The signer may get the message that help is needed and will re-sign that portion of the message. Such movements must however be appropriate by cultural standards as well as visible to the signer. For example, waving to get a signer's attention should "fit" the context. If sitting in close proximity to the signer, the wave should be from the wrist and not from the shoulder. If, however, the deaf person is up on stage and the interpreter is in the second row of the audience, the wave may include movement from the elbow or the shoulder, depending on the distance and the lighting.

Holding one's arms crossed in front of the body prevents one from responding quickly to a signer or asking for clarification. Subtle interruptions, which are sometimes necessary, become more obvious as a sudden "unfurling action" catches attention. In addition, the signer may perceive crossed arms as a sign that the interpreter is nervous, or argumentative. Even if one is experiencing such emotions, there is no reason to add to the stress of the situation by visibly conveying personal stress.

———— 📖 ————

40c.   The interpreter's hands copy the signer's signs.

Research shows that people move their hands naturally as they think. This unconscious behavior, however, conflicts with the interpretation process. If interpreters move their hands, even, for example, to copy the signer's signs, or to gesture, this movement can be unnerving to signers. The signer may think the interpreter is trying to get the signer's attention, when this is not the case.

40d. Gestures are distracting.

The body displays nervousness, through involuntary signs like sweating or body tics. Interpreters may also have habitual behaviors related or unrelated to nervousness. Nervous or habitual gestures must be controlled because they distract the audience or the signer. For example, twiddling one's thumbs or picking one's nails may signal to everyone who sees this behavior that the interpreter is bored or distracted.

40e. Head movements are inappropriate.

When movements of the head are incongruent with the signed message, deaf signers, who are not familiar with non-verbal communication used by English speakers, may think that the interpreter does not understand. They may also think that negative information is being presented in the target language instead of the positive comments the signer made. For example, it is natural in English for speakers to move their head left to right when they want to emphasize how good things are or how impressed they are with something. Non-deaf people might imagine the sound "Mmm, Mmm!" going with the gesture. The headshake from left to right might mean "That was a great movie!" However, a deaf signer might have the impression that the interpretation is negative – "That was an awful movie!" It might even be taken to mean that the interpreter was expressing dislike or disapproval of the lecture.

171

NOTE: Some head movements are appropriate. For instance, it is reassuring to the signer when interpreters nod their heads. This gesture lets signers know that their signing and thus the information they want to impart to the audience is understood.

41. **The appearance of the interpreter is appropriate for the context.**

Possible errors

41a. Clothes are distracting or inappropriate: The interpreter shows up in a T-shirt with a large logo on it.
41b. Hair is distracting: The interpreter's haircut is asymmetrical.
41c. Jewelry or accessories are distracting: The interpreter wears dark glasses, or has obvious body piercings.
41d. Hands or nails are distracting: The interpreter chooses dark colored nail polish.

Discussion

It may seem that an interpreter's appearance is unimportant, particularly if the person is not obvious to the audience because he or she is sitting as they work. Even in these situations interpreters may have to make their presence known. They are then seen not only by the signer but also the audience, and must have an appropriate professional appearance.

For interpreters "inappropriate" appearance is simply "distracting" or "eye-catching" appearance. Generally speaking, nothing about the interpreter's appearance should be marked or unusual in any way. Even a slightly distinguishing feature like a droopy mustache, can be distracting.

41a.   **Clothes are distracting or inappropriate.**

Interpreters must be aware of the setting they are working in and dress accordingly. It would be inappropriate, for example, to be wearing a dress and high heels at a construction site. The idea is to dress appropriately from head to toe. Members of an audience do notice appearance, and they may make judgements about the signer based on the interpreter's appearance. Deaf people often mention that footwear should match the apparel of the interpreter and the setting. If one is dressed nicely, dress shoes and not runners or winter boots should be worn.

Clothes should be suitable for the work context, and that context includes the signer's needs. For example, a fair skinned Caucasian interpreter would normally wear a dark shirt or top, for best visibility if they have to do some signing to the presenter. However, if the signer is visually impaired and prefers light clothes, a white shirt would be appropriate.

NOTE: If an interpreter's work is being assessed, any reasons for non-standard dressing should be explained to the person doing the assessment.

41b.　　Hair is distracting.

An interpreter's choice of hairstyle is very personal, and therefore, hard to assess. What is "distracting" to one person might not be "distracting" to another. However, if one's hairstyle is noticeable and significantly different from everyone else's in the context then the style may be inappropriate. Types of hairstyle that deaf people have noted as distractions include dyed hair with an unusual color such as pink or purple, asymmetrical hair cuts where one side is three inches longer than the other side, spiked hair or hair arranged in a Mohawk. In addition, facial hair such as long-handled mustaches or three-inch wide sideburns can also be considered distressingly eye-catching.

41c. Jewelry or accessories are distracting.

In this age of technology interpreters often arrive at assignments with cell phones and pagers attached to their waists or tucked in to pockets. If the devices start ringing or vibrating, they cause interpreters to lose their focus. These devices should not be visible, and they should also be turned off so that neither the interpreter, the signer, nor the audience is distracted. Tongue, nose and eye piercings, as well as tattoos that are visible, can be very distracting and should be avoided.

41d. Hands or nails are distracting.

Interpreters' hands are very important in their work. Very long, colorfully polished, or dirty, broken fingernails can be distracting. Even though it seems that the appearance of the hands is not important when interpreting from ASL to English, this is not so. The signer may be put off by any kind of visual distraction, just as non-deaf people might "notice" the lisp of a speaker. Interpreters, therefore, need to keep their nails a natural color.

Professional Organizations

Organizations in Canada

AVLIC
Association of Visual Language Interpreters of Canada
11337-61 Avenue
Edmonton, Alberta T6H 1M3
www.avlic.ca

CAD
Canadian Association of the Deaf
Suite 203, 251 Bank St.
Ottawa, Ontario K2P 1X3
www.cad.ca

CCSD
Canadian Cultural Society of the Deaf
House 144, 11337-61 Avenue
Edmonton, Alberta T6H 1M3
www.ccsdeaf.com

Organizations in the United States

ASLTA
American Sign Language Teachers Association
814 Thayer Ave
Silver Spring MD 20910-4500
www.aslta.org

CIT
Conference of Interpreter Trainers
www.cit-asl.org

NAD
National Association of the Deaf
814 Thayer Avenue
Silver Spring MD 20910-4500
www.nad.org

RID
Registry of Interpreters for the Deaf, Inc.
333 Commerce Street
Alexandria VA 22314
www.rid.org

Bibliography

Ailes, R. (1988). *You are the Message: Secrets of the Master Communicators.* Dow Jones-Irwin, Homewood, IL.

Armstrong, D., Stokoe, W., & Wilcox, S. (1995). *Gesture and the Nature of Language.* Cambridge University, Cambridge.

Association of Visual Language Interpreters of Canada (1988-1998). Proceedings of the Biennial Conferences of the Association of Visual Language Interpreters of Canada.

Bahan, B. (1996). Non-manual Realization of Agreement in American Sign Language. Unpublished doctoral dissertation, Boston University, MA.

Baker-Shenk, C. & Cokely, D. (1980). *American Sign Language: A Teacher's Resource Text on Grammar and Culture.* Gallaudet University, Washington, D.C.

Braden W. W. (Ed). (1961). *Speech Methods and Resources: A Textbook for the Teacher of Speech.* Harper and Brothers, NY.

Bragonier R., Jr. & Fisher, D. (Eds). (1981). *What's What: A Visual Glossary of Everyday Objects: From Paper Clips to Passenger Ships.* Random House, NY.

Brislin, R. W. (1981). *Cross-Cultural Encounters: Face to Face Interaction.* Pergamon, NY

Cokely, D. (1992). Interpretation: A sociolinguistic model. *Sign Language Dissertation Series.* Linstok Press, Burtonsville, MD.

Cokely, D. (Ed). (1992). *Sign Language Interpreters and Interpreting.* Linstok Press, Burtonsville, MD.

Colonomos, B. M. (1992). *Processes in Interpreting and Transliterating: Making Them Work for You.* The Bicultural Center, Riverdale, MD.

Conference of Interpreter Trainers. (1981 – 2000). Proceedings of the Biennial Conferences of Interpreter Trainers National Conventions.

Cooper, B. K. (1994). *Speak with Power: Six Steps & Eight Keys for Speaking Success.* Pow!–R Publications, Calgary, Alberta.

Crocker, L. & Algina, J. (1986). *Introduction to Classical and Modern Text Theory.* Holt, Rinehart & Winston, NY.

Crystal, D. (1987). *The Cambridge Encyclopedia of Language.* Cambridge University, NY.

Ellis, D. G. & Donohue, W. A. (Eds). (1986). *Contemporary Issues in Language and Discourse Processes.* Lawrence Erlbaum Associates, Hillsdale, NJ.

Frishberg, N. (1986). *Interpreting: An Introduction.* Registry of Interpreters for the Deaf, Alexandria, VA.

Gaskell, J. & McLaren, A. (1987). *Women and Education: A Canadian Perspective.* Detselig Enterprises, Calgary, Alberta.

Gregory, H. (1990). *Public Speaking for College and Career (2nd ed).* McGraw-Hill, NY.

Halliday, M. A. K. & Hasan, R. (1976). *Cohesion in English.* Longman, London.

Harrington E. C. (1999). *The Big Book of Beastly Mispronunciations: The Complete Opinionated Guide for the Careful Speaker.* Houghton Mifflin, NY.

Humphrey, J. H., & Alcorn, B. J. (1996). *So You Want to be an Interpreter: An Introduction to Sign Language Interpreting* (2nd ed). H & H Publishers, Amarillo, TX.

Johnston, T. (1991). Spatial syntax and spatial semantics in the inflection of signs for the marking of person and location in Auslan. *International Journal of Sign Linguistics*, 2 (1), 29-62.

Joos, M. (1967). *The Five Clocks*. Harbinger Books, NY.

Journal of Interpretation (1986-1999). Registry of Interpreters for the Deaf, Alexandria, VA.

Lieb, A. (1993). *Speaking for Success: The Canadian Guide*. Harcourt Brace Javanovich, Toronto.

Lucas, S. E. (1989). *The Art of Public Speaking* (3rd ed). Random House, NY.

McBurney, J. H. & Wrage, E. J. (1965). *Guide to Good Speech* (3rd ed). Prentice-Hall, Englewood, NJ.

Mitchell, A. (1973). *Speech Communication in the Classroom*. Pitman, NY.

Neumann Solow, S. (2000). *Sign Language Interpreting: A Basic Resource Book* (rev. ed). Linstok Press, Burtonsville, MD.

Ozolins, U. & Bridge, M. (1999). *Sign Language Interpreting in Australia*. Language Australia, Melbourne.

Petrone Stratiy, A. (1999). (Videotape) *You Think Deaf People have Problems?* Deaf Utopia, Edmonton, Alberta.

Registry of Interpreters for the Deaf (1982 – 1999). Proceedings of the Biennial National Conventions of the Registry of Interpreters for the Deaf.

Rivers, W. M. & Temperley, M. S. (1978). *A Practical Guide to the Teaching of English as a Second or Foreign Language*. Oxford University, NY.

Ross, R. S. (1965). *Speech Communication: Fundamentals and Practice.* Prentice-Hall, Englewood Cliffs, NJ.

Roy, C. (ed). (2000) *Innovative Practices for Teaching Sign Language Interpreters.* Gallaudet University, Washington, D.C.

Roy, C. (2000). *Interpreting as a Discourse Process.* Oxford University, NY.

Seal, B. C. (1998). *Best Practices in Educational Interpreting.* Allyn and Bacon, Boston, MA.

Seleskovitch, D. (1978). *Interpreting for International Conferences: Problems of Language and Communication.* Pen and Booth, Washington D.C.

Sign Language Research: Theoretical Issues. (1990). Gallaudet University, Washington D.C.

Sign Language Studies. (1978-1996). Linstok Press, Burtonsville, MD.

Stufflebeam, D. L. (1988). *The Personnel Evaluation Standards: How to Assess Systems for Evaluating Educators.* Sage Publications, Newbury Park, CA.

Supalla, S. (1992). *The Book of Name Signs: Naming in American Sign Language.* Dawn Sign Press, San Diego, CA.

Taylor, M. M. (1993). *Interpretation Skills: English to American Sign Language.* Interpreting Consolidated, Edmonton, Alberta.

Taylor, M. M. (1993). *Taylor's Diagnostic Assessment Instrument.* Interpreting Consolidated, Edmonton, Alberta.

184 Walter, O. M. & Scott, R. L. (1979). *Thinking and Speaking: A Guide to Intelligent Oral Communication.* Macmillan, NY.

Winston, E. A. (1993). Spatial Mapping in Comparative Discourse Frames in an American Sign Language Lecture. Unpublished doctoral dissertation, Georgetown University, Washington D.C.

Subject Index

Other Products from
Interpreting Consolidated

Textbook: Interpretation Skills: English to American Sign Language
(1993) by Marty M. Taylor ISBN: 0-9697792-0-8

Videotape: Pursuit of ASL: Interesting Facts Using Classifiers (1998)
with Angela Petrone Stratiy ISBN: 0-9697792-3-2